MAGICK OF THE ANCIENT GODS

Chthonic Paganism

&

The Left Hand Path

By Michael W. Ford

Houston, Texas

Michael W. Ford has authored the following books:

LUCIFERIAN WITCHCRAFT 2005

BOOK OF THE WITCH MOON 1999-2005

LIBER HVHI 2006

ADAMU 2006

LUCIFERIAN GOETIA 2007

BIBLE OF THE ADVERSARY 2007

FIRST BOOK OF LUCIFERIAN TAROT 2007

LUCIFERIAN TAROT 2007

GATES OF DOZAK – BOOK OF THE WORM 2008

SATANIC MAGICK – A PARADIGM OF THERION 2008

AKHKHARU – VAMPYRE MAGICK 2008

RITES OF THE ANTICHRIST –Art of Spiritual Lawlessness- 2009

MAGICK OF THE ANCIENT GODS

Chthonic Paganism & The Left Hand Path

MICHAEL W. FORD

MAGICK OF THE ANCIENT GODS
Chthonic Paganism & the Left Hand Path
By Michael W. Ford

Illustrations by Various classical sources reworked by Michael W. Ford.
Cover Art by Draconis @ demiurgegraphics@hotmail.com

ISBN 978-0-578-02732-6
First edition 2009 Succubus Productions

Succubus Productions
PO Box 926344
Houston, TX 77292
USA
Website: http://www.luciferianwitchcraft.com
email: succubusproductions@yahoo.com

By Torch-bearing Hekate,
I summon thee by blood,
by honey and by rose
Goddess of Howling Dogs
and Gorgon's cries
in the hours of night
Hekate Einodia, Trioditis,

To Zeus Keraunos, Astrapaios
O father Zeus,
who shakes with fiery light
the world above, deep-sounding
from thy lofty height.
From thee proceeds the
ethereal lightning's blazing eye,
the serpent unbound,
flashing around intolerable rays

MAGICK OF THE ANCIENT GODS

CHTHONIC PAGANISM & THE LEFT HAND PATH

I. Reestablishing the Gods

Paganism

Left Hand Path Paganism

The Difference of Luciferian Paganism and Magick

Gods and Goddesses

Gods and Humanity

Luciferian Epithets

II. Magick and Offerings

Olympian and Chthonic Ritual

Incense, Candles and Altars

Offerings and their Purpose

Example Offering

III.   Theos Epiphanes

Gods and Goddesses of Illumination and Victory

IV.   Theoi Khthonioi

Dark Gods & the Rituals of the Underworld

V.   Moon Phases and Witchcraft

Bibliography

Eosphorus, the Morning Star

FORWARD

Magick of the Ancient Gods is a grimoire in every way, it is meant to inspire and enchant those who read it, who may not know which path to embark upon and find the thought of the awakening of the Gods and Goddess mutually inspiring. This work began from a specific coin I had obtained due to my interest in Antiochus IV Epiphanes. The coin displayed the radiate head of Antiochus and the back Zeus bearing a lightning bolt. I had conducted numerous meditations with it – the age alone of the coin was from his lifetime – 175-164 B.C. and had survived since. The inspiration was blinding, I began researching the Gods even deeper than before and looked to the Adversarial spirit in each. My Daimon never leads me into a wrong direction; I found my wellspring and focus. I was to create a grimoire which was simplistic and easy to understand, where the workings and magickal rites could be conducted without extensive pressure and adapted by a beginner.

The Gods may be viewed here for the first time in a Luciferian and Left Hand Path perspective – there is no "Good" or "Evil" here, there is balance. No more will you see "Zeus" as being some equivalent to the Judeo-Christian God, rather a balanced force of power of both light and darkness. The Adversary manifests in each and every culture, as I have mentioned before yet not in the "devilish" way others seem to always accept.

Luciferianism is about knowledge and wisdom applied, *in different ways than first perceived*. I encourage each to explore these avenues no matter if you are a Wiccan or Satanist – you will find this grimoire illuminating in your own magickal search and awakening.

They exist now within our flesh; they travel through the labyrinth of dreams and seek a greater manifestation in our waking world. We may seek them in nature, our daily activities and goals.

There are many masks of the Adversary, all of which are different with various perspectives and possible goals for the practitioner to approach. The success of the work here is up to you desire and how Magick manifests in you as an individual.

The statues of the Gods, altars and tools of the art is a balance of the need of visual, perceptive elements without your life, a bridge as it is to this world and manifestation. The Gods offer their cups as well to those who may drink from them!

The path of Magick requires the ability to gain perspective from our experiences, to allow them to influence our shaping into Gods and Goddesses accordingly. Listen to nature and the world devoid of the bustle of technology once in a while, the beauty of nature itself will inspire you!

Michael W. Ford, Akhtya

May 13, 2009

PART I.

REESTABLISHING THE GODS

Temple of Zeus at Pergamum from "The Book of History".
This, along with the symbol of Serpents and the Basket on
Pergamum coins are what have been referred to as *The
Seat of Satan*. It is imperative to understand that
Luciferian Pagans do not believe in the "devil" necessarily
as a destructive or literal being, rather a symbol of our
shadow and unconscious desires as beings.

REESTABLISHING THE GODS

The Luciferian path has long been misinterpreted with modern "devil worship" and the supplication to a purely moralistic "evil" being who seeks to burn and torment souls. This type of a one-sided paradigm is responsive only to Judeo-Christian consideration, as Luciferians neither believe in a "devil" nor worship a one-sided being. Luciferians understand that humans are multi-sided and neither "black" nor "white". Judeo-Christian concepts that inspire ignorance and fear must have all of their "air" taken from their sails, never forgotten so that we must know what not to repeat.

Understanding Christianity is to know that no other religious culture has done more to destroy the Will and Mind of humanity than the cursed plague which spread throughout the late Roman Empire. Those who tried to stop it – Nero Caesar, Domitian, and Seleucid King Antiochus IV Epiphanies with Judaism (a religion of a specific sect of people) were proclaimed in their later works as agents of a "devil". The idea of Lucifer is far older than Christianity as is that of Ahriman or Angra Mainyu. We will present very little of this avenue of the left hand path, rather focusing on reestablishing the foundation of Paganism for Luciferian-minded individuals from all cultures and perspectives.

The Luciferian path is an establishment of the possibility of self-directed ascension or "god/goddess" making of the Luciferian. The path of this type of Paganism invokes the self-association of the Gods or Goddesses.

PAGANISM

Pagan means "country dweller" and is a general definition for pre-Christian beliefs and practices. Paganism transcends every culture and time before and after Christianity. The Neo-Pagan revival of the past 60+ years has proven eventful in breaking down Judeo-Christian ideals and reestablishing a way for people to re-connect with nature.

The problem is that in the attempt to stand out from Christianity, men and women have fought off and hidden the shadow and dark element, playing defense of Christians who point the finger and scream "devil-worshipper", all the while with the other hand holding their beer, gun or key to the flashy new car. Is it not Ironic that the religion of Christianity instructs the rejection of the shadow yet fully practices the degeneration of the very ideals upheld by them?

We will not push the dark gods away; we will embrace them as a part of ourselves. We connect to them in everything around us. Sometimes, we connect more than other times. Our offerings are honest and respectful of the ancient ways nearly forgotten.

You will find darkness here yet also the light of wisdom.

The Gods will inspire many things, you will even find out more about who you are. Closely aligned with nature, your antinomian path of self-deification may bring about a new level of initiatory knowledge and power.

LEFT HAND PATH PAGANISM

The Left Hand Path has long been a term relating to Satanism and "evil" in association with Judeo-Christian thoughts. What Luciferianism and Paganism is within the context of this work is a process of self-empowerment and transformation by smashing duality and establishing balance as a foundation of a spiritual, mental and physical journey in life. It is *antinomian*, or *against-the-law* of the spiritual mainstream as it is.

To be Luciferian and Pagan is to acknowledge that you are the vessel in which the Gods manifest, thus it is a deeply spiritual and physical experience. *Luciferian or Left Hand Path Pagans don't worship the Gods in sending love outwards – we direct our offerings inward to build ourselves accordingly.*

The term Lucifer as shown here in origins presents a God of Light, or a Goddess of Light. This is wisdom, enlightenment, balance and objectivity. The darker, daemonic or chthonic aspects are equally a part of our being and don't symbolize "evil" or "good", rather this is a process of building power and continued existence.

Power is the experience and temporary result of measured application of Wisdom and Action, with a specific Goal oriented activity to achieve something. **Luciferians view the Gods as models of character, to obtain wisdom and expand consciousness.** When we feel strong we thank the Gods which incarnate within us as a part of our being. When we feel weak we invoke or offer to the Gods which incarnate a path of self-determined strength. We don't grovel or pray to something outside, we don't adhere to a monotheistic religion which does not make reasonable sense to ourselves. We don't feel guilt or accept the notion of "sin", there are the pleasures of life and we should never harm another without a purpose of defense.

To be at one with your choice of God and Goddess, to make suitable offerings which neither degrade nor take away from your individuality, to empower yourself through visualizing the Gods as a part of yourself. Knowing both the beauty and ugliness of darkness and light, in turn seeking to balance them within your life, this is the path of the Luciferian Pagan. You will not "water" down nor "whitewash" any deity, fully exploring the shadow and the torch of illumination. With a bit of courage, you will know more about yourself and the possibilities in your life from such an undertaking.

For those who may not find specific resonance with traditional "Satanic" symbolism of the Western World, the foundational concepts of the Gods and Goddesses will no doubt fuel your passion of the origins of the Luciferian spirit.

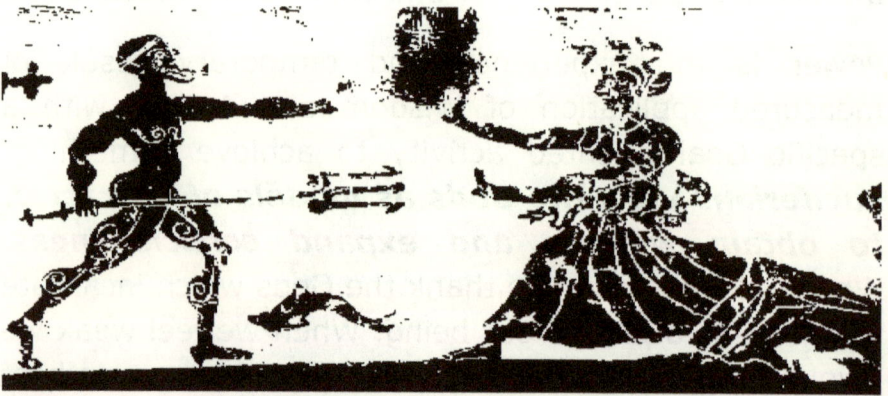

Poseidon and Medusa

THE DIFFERENCE OF LUCIFERIAN PAGANISM AND MAGICK

Magick occurs in every act, with every thought and event in your life. There is no spell written to describe the moment of crossing a threshold or boundary which brings that sense of ecstasy. Magick is the process of *compelling* change in your own universe, changing things often towards the betterment of your existence. Luciferian Magick is a discipline-oriented practice, creating extremely results-driven sorcerers who essentially become something Godlike and striving towards spiritual immortality, an existence beyond flesh or the survival of the psyche.

Practical Luciferian Magickians use the practice to shape their world and live here and not, not concerned with an afterlife. All Luciferians question everything and find what corresponds with their approach. Luciferian Magick focuses specifically on the darker Gods and Daemons from a multicultural and mythological perspective, yet never allowing the Christian ideology to pervert their workings. Many Luciferian Magickians work with the ancient Persian Yatuk Dinoih, or Daeva-yasna (called demon-worship), working closely with primal forces as a part of their own being, Ceremonial Ritual practice and even Goetia.

Luciferian Paganism embraces the exploration of the self through the Gods and Goddesses of many pantheons and cultures, the purpose of which is to elevate and shape your life according to your desire. This work is to be creative upon historical polytheism.

GODS & GODDESSES

Luciferianism is often associated with primal "devil-worship" or the supplication to a demonic figure, which cannot be further from the truth. If you view the Christian God as the one in the Bible, who is jealous, pours great wrath unto people everywhere, judges others and condemns spiritual freedom would he not be a devil? Luciferianism is a spiritual and material balance of the individual truly transforming the self in the image of a God or Goddess. This is a continual process which brings a deeper knowledge and intimate wisdom with the spiritual process and union with the forces of nature and other spiritual possibilities.

Light within itself is not the absolute, within all cultures, mythologies and throughout time Light is always balanced with Darkness to achieve completion and wisdom. The Adversary itself is a dual headed force which applies opposition to spiritual emptiness and one-sided deception. The Adversary embraces the darkness of the mind and the light of wisdom to expand his or her horizons in this world. For this reason alone, the followers of the Nazerene-doctrine label us "Evil" and "Satanic", yet in this world dominated by a Nazerene doctrine there is continual war, bloodshed and hate among all, all without balance due to the subconscious restriction of natural desire.

The Greek and Roman Gods present the Luciferian symbol as its standard. They exist within our subconscious and in the darkness of the soul and mind, they rise up as beautiful Gods and Goddesses to be as symbols of our potential and possibility, the daemons of darkness and war represent our wrath and vengeance as conscious individuals. Each God and Goddess possess both a daemonic/demonic and divine mask, it is up to the Luciferian on how they utilize the force itself.

GODS AND HUMANITY

To explain the consistency of the application of the Luciferian Path in relation to paganism and "living it" I would like to provide an example of a manifestation of this path. Two of the specific examples are indeed Luciferian individuals based on the following:

1. Both choose to shape their own destiny, even when odds were against them.

2. Both used cunning and planning to achieve what they wish.

By definition, individuals who seek to empower their lives and through antinomian self-deification manifest themselves as living Gods or Goddesses. This is Luciferian as the polytheistic use of Gods or Epithets is central to the Luciferian mind being able to balance darkness and light according to their own design in life.

Mythology often presents the balance of initiation of humanity; often they are too insensitive to understand the deeper considerations. While Zeus has battled with the Giants, Titans and more, he is deeply connected to them as they are to him. Aspects of each dwell within our deep subconscious. As a Luciferian, you must never fall prey to comparing the Gods to the Christian-value system, for such is for slaves and the ignorant, unknowing fools. If you venerate Zeus as the bringer of power to yourself, offer incense and what you will, yet also offer to Hades and the keeper of the knowledge and power within the depths of your soul. Honor as many Gods as you wish, for they incarnate within your flesh.

The Gods and Daimons all are depicted anthropomorphically in accordance with their desire or intent of the moment, much like we change our clothes to go to one event or another. When offerings, rituals or other visualization workings are practiced, it is a suitable practice to see them within your mind's eye or imagination.

To understand the symbolism of Zeus with relation to *"God Manifest"* or *"Theos Epiphanes"*, it is significant to study a relation to leadership and the manifestation of destined by Willed action. Usurping the Throne or in modern day action achieving victory over an area in your life often requires cunning and the application of strategy into action. This type of bold action be it personal, professional or otherwise will carry your path directly to victory or ruin.

Antiochus IV Epiphanes was the brother of Seleucus Philopater. Antiochus was raised partially in Rome, his Greek study and heritage aided him well in Rome as he grew accustomed to the methods of power applied by the hierarchy there, no doubt establishing in his mind a greater understanding of Luciferian – or – "the self as God" and destiny made manifest through Will.

Antiochus (his birth name is suggested to be Mithridates) traveled to Athens, Greece and became not only an Athenian citizen, yet also was elected to the chief magistracy. He soon found himself playing at being the successor of Pericles and would have most likely been successful until the assassination of Seleucus Nicator presented an opportunity.

Eumenes II of Pergamon and his brother Attalus invited Antiochus IV to Pergamum and offered to support him in taking the crown of the Seleucid Empire, for which Antiochus agreed. Both Eumenes and Attalus with an army of Pergamum escorted Antiochus from the Eastern road of Asia minor to Syria. Antiochus entered Syria and usurped the throne as his own. Knowing the challenges which faced him – family rivals, supporters of the Egyptian dynasty all stacked the odds against him as it would seem.

Antiochus knew this was a careful balance of like the Gods would play in times before. Antiochus must use guile with calculated and careful bloodshed. Antiochus had the petty would-be prince Heliodorus vanish to never be heard of again, Apollonius retired, Hyrcanus committed suicide and there was only the infant son Seleucus/Onias to deal with. Antiochus employed an assassin named Andronicus to kill the infant to secure his throne, which he did. Once the child was removed, Antiochus had Andronicus put to death for treason.

Like Zeus, Antiochus was a usurper as well. Usurpers can be seen as the ultimate Luciferians or manifestations of Gods, they choose to empower themselves and divinity by taking by force and will. This is one method of applying the Gods within your own life, to have them act through you by your actions in life.

Diana-Artemis, the Huntress

LUCIFERIAN EPITHETS

An Epithet is a description of a specific deity and the role in which they are applied. For instance, Apollo has many epithets, as the Lord of Death or Plaque spreader he is called *Apollo Far-Striker*, as the leader of muses he is *Apollo Musagetes.* Zeus also has many epithets as his role is deep and varied as well. *Zeus Lykios* is his name as the Wolf-God, which is described later in this tome.

Luciferian Epithets are present throughout the works of Luciferian Witchcraft, Akhkharu, The Bible of the Adversary, Liber HVHI, The First Book of Luciferian Tarot and much more. The Adversary is presented in numerous roles, thus as the more illuminated or "angelick" aspects are explored and presented here.

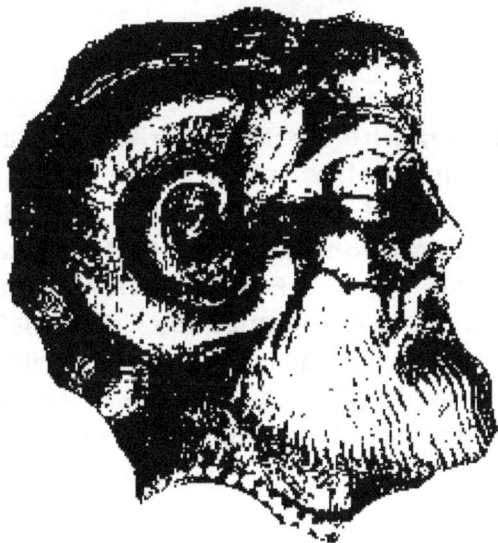

Zeus Ammon

Emperor Domitian, who resisted Christianity and fought to keep the Pagan spirit alive, shown here from a Roman coin. It was the brother of Domitian, Titus who destroyed the temple in Jerusalem. Domitian, who had a macabre sense of humor, often held "Death Feasts" where Roman senators were invited to be accompanied by "demons" or children painted black and carrying death-plaques with their names upon them. It was dangerous to be an Emperor as so many were killed, assassinated or deposed by plots by Senators.

II. MAGICK AND OFFERINGS

Emperor Nero, who identified himself with Apollo, the god of healing and the plague, the far-shooter, Hekatebolos who was Helios incarnate. Nero, who fought Christian ignorance, is shown here in a bust with roman armor, lion-heads and medusa upon his breastplate.

OLYMPIAN and CHTHONIC RITUAL

The two aspects of Luciferian Paganism with relation to Magick or initiation into the mysteries you will find Olympian, or the Empyrean/High aspects relating to the Gods of Mount Olympia, generally light bringing more self-strengthening rites, visualize Spring and Summer and Chthonic Rituals or the Underworld focusing on the infernal Daimonic Gods as sorcerous illumination. Visualize autumn and winter, both aspects are essential and should be explored even if ones "natural association" is not found in one. You may "keep it simple" with basic offerings and not go further into Magick as initiation or fully embrace the process of self-deification and antinomian self-empowerment. If so, Luciferianism as from The Bible of the Adversary and Luciferian Witchcraft would increase and strengthen your understanding.

When you perform an offering, invocation or prayer reflecting to the self take a moment to visualize the God or Goddess, specifically from the statue or idol before you. This is merely an object of focus and is a reflection of that which you attain to become. You will find the more belief invested in the process the more results attained.

With Luciferian practice, you will consider the approach of any type of rite conducted. Initially, all Olympian or Empyrean rites the burnt offering / incense is made to ascend upward to the Gods, offerings to the Gods of Darkness or the Underworld was generally forbidden. Luciferians see the word 'forbidden' as being 'test' therefore to gleefully rebel and experience. Gods are created in the act of independent thinking and rebellion, yet it is a path of pain and struggle – yet the act is worth it along with the result.

INCENSE, CANDLES & ALTARS

Traditionally throughout the ancient Greek and Seleucid Empire Frankincense was used on every altar throughout the empires, it was the foundation of worship and aromatic offering. Myrrh was also highly prized throughout the Seleucid Empire and used religiously. The primary incense for use is Frankincense, Myrrh and even Cinnamon, depending on your personal preference.

Candles should be the color according to the rite and the nature of the God and Offering. Light blue should not be used for cursing rituals or seeking the wisdom of Hades like Black would, green would be used for nature workings, job advancement or the like. Yellow is for health and red for pleasure, love, etc. Altars may be simple, small decorated with the image of the God. You may find reasonable small statues to take center upon your altar. If where you live has some rural aspects to it, you may make a small earthen altar at a tree or someplace suitable to the God or Goddess. If it is a God of Water, you may place it next to a river, only make sure that none would come by and take the statue!

OFFERINGS AND THEIR PURPOSE

Offering and praying to the Gods is simply a reference to coming into spiritual contact with your inner guides and a chance to focus your spiritual directives. If you believe in the spiritual existence of the Gods in any form, this definition means little yet will allow you to achieve the same end. Prayers and offerings are a meaningful and simplistic way to invoke a sense of the consciousness within you.

The Offering model here is a simple prayer in which it is done according to Roman and Greek tradition. The ceremonial or ritual aspect as within the Luciferian Path or Magickal tradition itself does not transpire deeply into it. Many individuals wish only a way to honor the Gods and Goddesses without the constraints of ritual workings involving a significant amount of time.

Some will use prayers rarely as empowerment focusing, from an Atheistic viewpoint, some will use prayers as a frequent religious focus, a daily exercise as devotionals. A Luciferian may conduct both ways yet the focus must always remain towards self-empowerment, viewing your body and mind as the Temple or Vessel of the Gods. After all, your consciousness itself is a Gift of Prometheus, the Light Bringer or in out-side Roman and Greek traditions, Luciferian Black Flame.

The Luciferian creates an altar space with symbols of his or her chosen deific masks, or Gods/Goddesses. Use the incense, invocations and candles which are symbolic to the specific God in which you are focusing on. A Luciferian who does not intend to practice 'in-depth' rituals or workings may wish to provide offerings/libations to the Gods of his or her own choice.

EXAMPLE WORKING

A following example is a suitable offering:

Prayer symbol: Touch left hand to forhead, reciting quietly the name of Deific Mask (or God/Goddess)

When: Night of Full Moon

God/Goddess offered to: Hecate

Purpose (Spiritual) – To give thanks for insight.

Purpose (Material/personal) – to acquire further awareness & instinctual insight.

Offering: Honey and Rose Water, incense of Hecate, single white candle

Prayer: *"I call to thee Triple Moon Goddess Hecate, who guards and presides over the crossroads and graveyard, who holds the power of entry into the realm of manes, I offer thee incense to honor your spirit, I offer thee honey and rose water to offer to your eyes which look upon my path and bless it with power. Hecate, by the Maiden, by the Mother and by the Crone bestow unto me the Wisdom of your Spirit, that I may hold both the wisdom and knowledge of darkness and light, Accept this offering"*

Pour offering when you reference it in prayer, lift hands up when making reference to incense. Take a moment to look at the Moon and enjoy the night atmosphere, visualize the spirit of Hecate in its various forms – as the howling of dogs, wolves the sound of owls. If the ritual is darker in nature, adapt the prayer to an invocation of Hecate as the Goddess of Black Witchcraft, depending on your desire.

Offering at Temple of Apollo

CONCERNING INVOCATIONS

The invocations are adapted from the ancient Orphic and Homeric hymns, prayers and traditional offerings. They have been adapted to be recited in our contemporary time. They will be as effective as you make them. When offering, believe and fully visualize the Gods and your goals, see them being manifest in you and as you act during the day and night, these powers shall incarnate according to your actions.

Often, using a combination of prayers or invocations with the process of "speaking in tongues" or reciting "mantras" will create feelings of high energy and ecstasy, use methods like this to "get in tune" with your invocations and offerings.

The word invocation means 'to call inward' and thus represents a centering or union of the Godform with the mind. All magickal workings or rituals should be conducted in a way to which you feel "at one" with the force invoked.

One of the most intense ways of ensuring success in the operation of invocation, simply "invoke" with a frenzy, believing every word at every moment, allow your mind to be lost in the act and do not think of anything else. Once the invocation has been completed, you may focus on your goal at hand.

III. THEOS EPIPHANES

GODS AND GODDESSES OF ILLUMINATION AND VICTORY

Helios, the Sun

ZEUS

The might of Zeus is beyond that of all the Gods, for he is known as "The Cloud Gatherer", "The Rejoicer in Thunder" and "The Aegis-Bearer". His mastery in the Wind, his great weapon is lighting and is the mark of his inspiration. Zeus battled the Titans and Typhon to achieve mastery over his higher state of being.

Zeus is the King of the Gods, the empyrean god of the sky and fate. His regal form was a mature man, bearded, sturdy and strong with a dark beard. He usually held a royal scepter, eagle and lightning bolt.

Zeus created the balance between the Empyrean and Infernal realms by placing the titans in Tartaros. This underworld is essential in understanding the hidden desires, strengths and power of each individual. For truly does both Zeus and Hades both hold sway within the psyche of humanity.

It was Zeus who deified his favored son Herakles, who was ascended to Olympos upon his death. It is said that Zeus dwells among the highest mountain peaks, his darker associations being with Zeus Lykios, the Wolf God who enjoys the devoured flesh of humans.

Zeus holds great respect among the council of Gods, it is even Poseidon who stands in respect when Zeus enters the Golden chambers of the Temple in Olympos. As the form of King, Zeus shows him Enthroned in splendor and holding in his left hand the scepter and winged lightning, his right hand holding out with a bowl to receive the offerings of his worshippers.

Zeus Nikephorus, who took the throne by force according to his chosen desire and destiny.

To worship the Gods in to honor their attributes in yourself, thus you become God-Incarnate or **Theos Epiphanes**, *the Living God Manifest*. Long ago was this title for Kings, rulers of people, yet now in such times is the torch available to those able to perceive its responsibility and potential by lifting up the self to the heights of the empyrean and the depths of the infernal realm.

Gods are measured by their ability to grow, command and overcome alone, never by birthright in times such as this! The Luciferian who may name his or her path and command it to flesh in this world is in the physical aspect God incarnate, balanced with a spiritual path of growth in acknowledging you are the only god that is will attend to the path of immortality of the antinomian psyche of self.

It was Zeus who was most honored by Antiochus IV Epiphanes, during his conflict with the Jews he placed the statue of Zeus upon their altar and insist offerings be made.

Zeus was indeed the one who willed Order in the universe, yet fully understood the nature of chaos and the need for darkness and disorder. He ruled fairly, often with kindness yet at other times harshly and without mercy. In subduing the Immortal Giants or Titans Zeus calmed and placed these old gods in the pits of Tartaros or the abyss to rest at his command.

Upon claiming the Kingship of the World and Gods, Zeus rode a four-horsed chariot to Olympus and set in place other Gods and Goddess to rule with him. The Luciferian who understands the essence of balance knows that such symbols of power, either Chthonic or Olympian does not designate weakness by any measure, it merely is a process of consciousness and transformation.

The colors attributed to Zeus is green and blue, his sacred animal being the Eagle. When winter beings the month is sacred to Maimakterion being Zeus Maimaktes. The interesting Egyptian-oriented God "Zeus-Serapis" features a seeming union with Hades, having the Cerebus at his side. Zeus in this form is truly "Adversarial" as he holds power to both the Empyrean or Olympian and Infernal or Chthonian.

Zeus Serapis was an Egyptian God which unified Zeus and Helios as the Sun God, sovereign power, Dionysos for nature, Hades for the Underworld and Afterlife and Aesculapius the art of healing.

Zeus Olympios was the supreme God of the Heavens and Sky, over other Gods. His power, embodied in an individual is powerful in this world and the outlook in which it may assist the Luciferian. A great temple was funded by Antiochus IV Epiphanes to be built in Greece dedicated to this god and is featured on the back of coins as well.

Zeus Nikephoros from Antiochus IV Epiphanes coin

Zeus Nikephoros is the epithet of Zeus "Bearer of Victory". This is the Great Hellenic God which conquers all which confronts him.

Zeus Xenios was placed and erected in Samaria to displace the Jehovah in Shechem. Zeus Xenios is the God of Hospitality and guests.

Zeus Aegiochos is the terror-inspired God who brings fear to his enemies.

Antiochus IV Epiphanes as Zeus

Zeus Ammon was the God which conquered and was adopted by Alexander the Great. Alexander the Great is featured on many coins with the Horns of Ammon meaning power, knowledge and kingship. In a Luciferian perspective, this relates to self-deification.

The Christian Bible specifically attributed Zeus to Satan as well. In Revelation 2:13 the writer makes association to Pergamum / Pergamon as being the location of the "Throne of Satan". "*I know where you live—where*

Satan has his throne. Yet you remain true to my name. You did not renounce your faith in me, even in the days of Antipas, my faithful witness, who was put to death in your city—where Satan lives." – Zeus was the Lord of Gods who would not allow the Judeo-Christian sheep herding god to further corrupt his lands and kingdom on earth. It is a shame that the Roman world later adopted this bastard faith – it simply attempted to kill culture and myth and replace it with a lesser, weaker one which instructed consistent obedience.

Zeus Olympios Nikephoros, the patron god of Antiochus IV Epiphanes reign of the Seleucid Empire.

A PRAYER TO ZEUS

PRAYER OF CALLING:

I call unto Kronides Hypatos (the Son of Kronos, Most High), I invoke thee Zeus, chief among the gods and greatest, all-seeing, the lord of all

the fulfiller who whispers words of wisdom to Themis as she sits leaning towards him. Be gracious, all-seeing Kronides, most excellent and great among the Gods, I offer thee libations for you to open your eyes through me!

O Zeus, much-honored father, Zeus supremely powerful and balanced, to thee my rites we consecrate, my prayers and expiations, king divine.

Hence mother earth (*gaia*) and mountains swelling high proceed from thee, the deep and all within the sky.

Kronion king, descending from above, commanding, sceptred Zeus!

Zeus Seraphis, Zeus-Hades-Dionysos with Cerebus

INVOCATION OF ZEUS

LORD OF THUNDER & LIGHTNING

(for prayers to self in striking forth and overcoming your challenges)

To Zeus Keraunos *(Thundering)* Astrapaios (*Lightning Maker*).

O father Zeus, who shakes with fiery light the world above, deep-sounding from thy lofty height.

From thee proceeds the ethereal lightning's blazing eye, the serpent unbound, flashing around intolerable rays.

Thy sacred thunders shake the blest abodes empyrean, the shining regions of the immortal Gods. You remind of them, As above, So below!

I call the mighty, splendid light, aerial, dreadful-sounding, fiery-bright, ethereal light, with angry voice, lighting through clouds with crashing power to fulfill my desire upon this earth!

Thy power divine the flaming lightning shrouds with dark investiture in fluid clouds, thou God of Inspiration and the Wisdom of Balance, I call to thee to empower and resound my weapons of Mind and Will, that I shall achieve my desire!

To You, Zeus Keraunos Astrapaios to brandish thunders strong and dire, to scatter storms, and dreadful darts of fire;

With roaring flames involving all around, and bolts of thunder of tremendous sound.

Thy rapid dart can raise the hair upright, and shake the heart of man with wild affright. Sudden, unconquered, holy, thundering God of the Winds, with noise unbounded flying all abroad

With all-devouring force, entire and strong, horrid, untamed, thou rollest the flames along.

Rapid, ethereal bolt, descending fire, the earth, all-parent, trembles at thine ire; the sea all-shining, and each beast, that hears the sound terrific, with dread horror fears: when nature's face is bright with flashing fire, and in the heavens resound they thunders dire.

They thunders white the azure garments tear, and burst the veil of all-surrounding air.

O Zeus, all-blessed, may thy wrath severe, hurled in the bosom of the deep appear, and on the tops of mountains be revealed, for thy strong arm is not from us concealed. Propitious to these sacred rites incline, and to thy suppliants grant a life divine,

I offer to thee to rise up through me, Theos Epiphanes!!

-Adapted from from the Ophiric Hymns

The Darker Invocations to Zeus are presented in the next chapter.

APOLLO / PHOIBOS APOLLO

One of the Greatest of the Gods, whose ability for prophecies and oracles made him one of the most powerful and diverse of the powers. Apollo held powers of Music, Plague spreading and death causing, poetry and archery as well as a protector of the young. Apollo is depicted as handsome young man, clean shaven who plays a lyre and sits upon a throne with a bow and arrow with a raven. Perhaps provided a foundation for the mask of "Lucifer" in the later Christian church, Apollo is indeed a balanced deific mask and God of the intelligent and insightful. An epithet of Apollo is Phoibos, meaning "bright one".

Apollon is the son of Zeus and Leto, a twin of Artemis. There is a description of him which draws association to Lucifer as the Angel of Light:

Philostratus the Younger, Imagines 14:

"Here is the god Apollon, painted as usual with unshorn locks; he lifts a radiant forehead above eyes that shine like rays of light."

Described by *Philostratus the Elder;*

"As for the aspect of the god Apollon, he is represented as unshorn, my boy, and with his hair fastened up so that he may box with girt-up head; rays of light rise from about his brow and his cheek emits a smile mingled with wrath; keen is the glance of his eyes as it follows his uplifted hands"

Herein we have a God of Light yet who also has a sinister or shadow side to his being. His close association to Helios perhaps may be an epithet for an aspect of Apollo. Within the concept of agriculture, Apollo was the essence of the bright and warming sun after the days of gloom and rain. Apollo had the ability to oversee horses and herds, being a protector.

Pestilence, it is said that Apollo had the power to avert locusts and mice, if he so desired. His shadow self or sinister aspect often presented him utilizing this power to send forth locusts as he wished as well. Apollo slayed the serpent in which he later regretted it, offering hymns when he may. It seems that Apollo's power increased when he was able to subdue the serpent, thus offering a suggestion of his controlling his primal urges and desires as the later Daemon-Prince Apollyon the Angel of the Bottomless Pit.

Apollo may be offered to for several purposes; those seeking divinization or direction, using the tarot, dreams and understanding.

Apollo Kitharoedos holding lyre from Antiochus IV Epiphanes Coin.

Apollo with Arrow and Bow upon Ompalos from Antiochus IV Epiphanes coin. The Ompalos is from the Delphian "Omphalos" which is a Baetyl, a house of the God and relates to the seat of divinity.

AN INVOCATION TO PHOIBOS APOLLO

(for workings of inspiration and knowledge)

I call unto thee, Phoibos Apollon,

of you even the swan sings with clear voice to the beating of his wings,

and of you the sweet-tongued minstrel,

holding lyre, always sings both first and last.

Hail to you lord! I seek your favor with my prayer.

I call to Apollon.

Blest Paian, come, propitious to my prayer, illustrious power,

God of Health, Lykoreus, Phoibos, fruitful source of wealth: Pytheion, golden-lyred, the field from thee receives its constant rich fertility.

Titan, Gryneion, Smyntheus, thee I call to rise up within me,

Delphion king: light-bearing Daimon

I offer unto thee Mousagetos (Leader of the Mousai),

O powerful King, whose light-producing eye views all within, and all beneath the sky;

Whose locks are gold, whose oracles are sure,

Who omens good reveals,

Who rises from and beyond the darkness,

Starry-eyed, profound,

To you, Apollo, all nature's music to inspire with harmonious lyre

The immortal golden lyre, now touched by thee,

All nature's tribes to thee their difference owe, and changing seasons from thy music flow:

Hence by mankind Pan royal, two-horned immortal named,

Shrill howling winds tearing through the syrinx famed;

Hear me, blest power, and in these rites rejoice,

Grant me the wisdom I seek, In your name through me, Hail!

AN OFFERING TO PYTHIAN APOLLO

(for divination workings, gaining inner wisdom)

I call unto thee, divine-inspired Apollo

Playing upon the golden hollow lyre

Clad and devouring the divine, risen in light of self-love

Strengthened in the Sun of your own recognized divinity!

Shine through me O Apollo Guardian of the Wise!

Swift as thought, rush from earth to Olympus

Go forth to the House of Zeus

Undying God of Light, Beauty and the Mysteries of the Dark veiled

It was you, Phoebus Apollo, who laid the foundations anew

Of a Great Temple unto which the Oracle shall divine

A future most desired and feared

Grant me the counsel of your singing, beautiful lyre

And a calm voice upon a soft breeze

Rise up through me and shall I be a glorious temple to you

For which I am the God which is manifest

The Eyes of Zeus and Hades ring out through my being

Yet we are one, I invoke and offer to thee

Apollo far-shooter, for you alone walk in the House of Zeus

And make all Gods tremble at your approach!

DIONYSOS

Dionysos, a God who had his roots in the east, was commonly associated with the lion, bull and was to be found in groves. His spirit was found in ecstatic intoxication, for he is the God of Wine and pleasure. He is known also as Bacchus (Bakchos) whose rites are filled with noise, kettle drums pounding; his rites are frenzied and inspiring.

The items associated with Dionysos is the Thyrsos, a pine-cone tipped staff, a leopard and drinking cup. Satyrs and nymphs attend him, rejoice in his power and spread forth his powers of ecstasy and revelry. Dionysos is inhibition liberated the very rejoicing of life and the pleasures of the spirit and flesh.

Dionysos appears in two forms, either a beaded man and to others as a youthful man who is the lover of Ariadne. Being the God of Awakening, his power is found in the psyche liberated, the very individual who is aware and stimulated in the world – hence the lack of restriction. His spirit is Luciferian by the ecstasy of life itself.

His power is great in the time of spring, when life emerges anew and flowers begin yet again. It was in the times of winter that Dionysos was dead, yet come spring, he arose from death as he was empowered by and inspires spring and summer.

Sigil Mask of Dionysos

The Priestesses of Dionysos, called "Thyiades", would be clothed in fawnskin covers, hair disheveled, holding the thyrsos and often holding serpents. They sought to rouse the infant Dionysos from his cradle, bringing forth spring upon the mountainside. Dionysos would spring forth in full form, in a rushing ecstasy would according to myth, capture anything living, tear it apart and devour it – human or animal.

Dionysos, fierce and sensual God of Intoxication & Pleasure

Dionysos was viewed in the summer as full of life, mature and strong. His gift was seen in the blossoming and overgrowth of trees and vines. The burning sun which dries up the greenery is Lykoirgos, it chases away Dionysos so that he goes forth to the sea, where he is taken by the Goddess Thetis who takes care until his time to rise again.

Some of the earliest worshippers of Dionysos called him by the title "**Omestes**", meaning "Raw Eater" for he would consume and devour flesh of both humans and animals. One of the last known instances of human sacrifice was recorded before the battle of Marathon in which two Persian captives were sacrificed to Dionysos.

Over time Dionysos was accepted as an Olympian God and was worshipped throughout Greece, officially. His Priests and Priestesses would become ecstatic and joyful; being able to hold dangerous serpents and other beasts not normally interacted with by man.

Dionysos demonstrated in mythology to have a considerable appreciation for the application of cruelty. He went to Argos and when people would not pay him honor, he drove their women mad and within the mountains he inspired the women to feed on the flesh of the babies suckling at their breasts.

Dionysos is depicted throughout myth and legend as a God illuminated, lifted from human frame to divinity through his own Will and sacred madness. Pentheus in Bacchae referenced Dionysos as a wizard, a sorcerer from the land of Lydia who had golden locks and burning eyes like Aphrodite's melting fire.

Dionysos-Bacchus upon lion

The beasts of the field were submissive and respectful of Dionysos, his eyes are described as Black in some cases, being able to cause vines and greenery to grow about and even restrain. Dionysos like Zeus is associated with Pergamum and the *"Throne of Satan"*. On a Greek silver Tetradrachm which is over 2,100 years old, the "Seat of Satan" is suggested by the Apostle John as being located in Pergamum/Pergamon and on it is the symbol of Dionysos. A basket featuring a snake coming from it was used in processions to honor the God of Pleasure and Excess, which the prudish and restrictive Christians associated with Satan or destructive behavior. Luciferians recognize Satan as a symbol for deeper knowledge and self-liberation from restrictive thought, blind faith and the Nazerene sickness so long infecting humanity. Dionysos instructs balance rather than pure consistent excess, this is the test of the God and some do not pass it, thus falling prey to the power of the Satyr-Father.

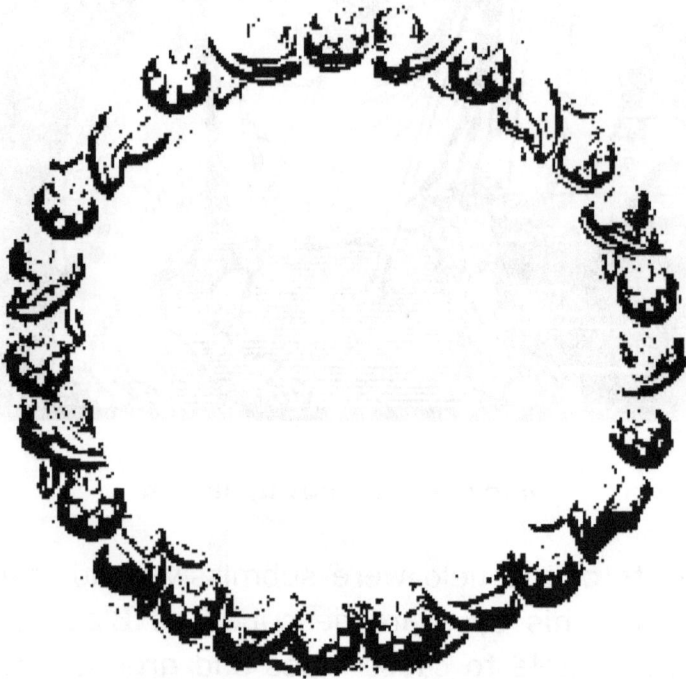

Wreath of Dionysos composed of leaves and berries from coin of Mithridates VI Dionysos

INVOCATION OF DIONYSOS

(for workings of carnal desire, focus and inner strength)

I invoke thee, Dionysos the ivy-crowned, *eribromos*,

Splendid son of Zeus and glorious Semele.

Come thou forth, inspire my dreams and mind, blessed Dionysos,

Bull-faced, begotten from thunder

Bakkhos famed. Bassaros God of universal might

Whom swords and blood and sacred rage delight

In heaven rejoicing, mad, furious inspiring God

Thou Dionysos, who dwells among humankind,

I invoke thy essence unto me, grant me the ecstasy I seek

Grant me the wisdom of your dreams, Hail thou Bacchus

Dionysos, thou divine, inspiring God, a twofold shape is yours

I invoke you by your names: O protogonos (firstborn),

trigonos (thrice begotten),

Bakkheion Lord of Violent Nature unbound!

Ineffable two-horned, with ivy crowned,

Bearer of the vine, endued with counsel divine

Eubouleos, whom the leaves of vines adorn,

Of Zeus and Persephoneia born in beds ineffable;

All-blessed power, Dionysos Risen!

Immortal Daimon, hear my call and hearken!

PART TWO

Burn Incense, Drink of Wine from Chalice, recite your prayer or desire. The following affirmation may be utilized to focus and hold association with the God itself.

AFFIRMATION OF DIONYSOS

Bakkhos phrenetic, bull-horned,

Lernaion, bearer of the vine;

From blackened fire descended,

Nysion king, from whom thy hidden rites spring.

Liknitos, fiery bright

Eubouleos crown-bearer, wandering forth in the night;
Bearing a scepter,

Omadion, captor, of a fiery light, born of Adversarial
Spirit,

Amphietos birght; love, mountain-wandering, clothed
with skins of the beast,

Paian golden-rayed, whom all revere,

Great annual god of grapes, the ivy crowned, .

Dionysos, theos taurokeros (*bull-horned god*),

Whom Zeus adorned him with crowns of snakes

Come, blessed power, regard thy voice, propitious
come,

And in these rites rejoice

So it is done.

THE RITUAL OF SPRING

An Invocation to Dionysos from the Chthonic Realms

Khthonion Dionysos, hear my prayer,

My invocation of thy spirit from sleeping realms,

Rise strong with Nymphai of lovely hair

Bakkhos Amphietos, God of life and ecstasy,

Who laid asleep in Persephone's abode, her sacred seat,

Whose knowledge of darkness is deep in the dreams of satyrs unbound

As with the memories of thy priestess chanting thy mystic songs

Rejoicing and rising in power

Come by widdershins and the power against the circle right

Come thou Dionysos, horned and divine

Accept my incense and prayer

Raise thy spirit in the earth and greenery around us

O thou Dionysos, thyrsus-bearing, with unshorn locks,

Perpetually young,

Who carries thy vine-clad spear

With a turban rakaina thy horned head

Adorned in robes of purple and gold,

Who beared visage appears at Will

So it is done.

SABAZIUS

Sabazius / Sabasius is a Thracian and Phrygian god who primary association was with Dionysus. Sabazius is a name of Dionysus which he assumed after coming to Phrygia and being initiated into the mysteries by Cybele. In common lore Sabazius was called by the Greeks a son of Zeus by Persephone.

Sabazius with serpents

Sabazius was worshiped in Athens and was honored in private mysteries along with Demeter and Persephone. The most significant symbol of the cult of Sabazius was a snake, a chthonian symbol of the underworld, wisdom and rebirth. It was said that small snakes coiled about the hands of his worshippers and that a representation of Sabazius is a crown of two small snakes raising their heads from which the God and his initiated members wore. The Cult of Sabazius like Cybele utilized music and players of double flutes and castanets with dancers lost in the chaos-inspired widdershins of ecstasy.

INVOCATION OF SABAZIUS

For the Rites of Summer, Pleasure and Serpentine Wisdom

I invoke thee, Sacred Sabazius, Dionysos-Risen God of serpents

Illustrious father, Daemon famed

Hail thy spirit of Bacchus, Bearer of the Vine

Thy divine spirit incarnate!

When mature, Dionysoian God of Serpent's entwined

Burst forth from thy concealed abode

Out of the Underworld, God of Light and Darkness

To sacred Tmolus, what delight!

Where Ippa dwells, the beauty and illuminated spirit!

Come thou Blessed Phrygian God, Devil-King on earth

Whose test is rarely passed, when image is surpassed

Great Saturn's offspring, Thou Sabazius

Whose serpent crown is adorned

TYCHE

TYKHE or Tyche is known as the Greek Goddess of Luck, she is Eutykhia, the Goddess of Good Luck and fortune. Tyche as she is often called was respected and worshipped as one of the Moiroi or Fates in ancient mythology.

She was known in not only Greece yet also the entire Middle East; specifically where the Seleucid Empire had established their rule and the Parthian Empire took over. Her shadowside or companion often shown in art is Nemesis; they are able to commonly decided good or bad misfortune for others. Tyche was featured on a coin of Parthian King Phraates IV, whom was feared as a ruler for killing his father and brothers to sustain his power. He remained King during Augustus Caesar.

Gotarez II enthroned receiving diadem from Tyche. Gotarez II was a Parthian King who assassinated his brother, Vardanes I to gain the Parthian throne. His portrait here shows him receiving glories from Tyche on a coin.

Conducting offerings to Tyche is a simple yet focused task. It is wise to bring kind offerings such as rose petals, incense and to meditate upon your course of action which will assist your fortune in the favor you desire beforehand. Tyche is best approached with your affirmation of intent and what you will do yourself along with the offering.

If you achieve something desired in life – be it a promotion, something you have worked hard for then you may wish to offer incense, smoke or such to Tyche to honor the victory.

AN OFFERING TO TYCHE

I offer to thee, O Goddess Tykhe,

Fumigation from Frankincense

Approach, Queen Tykhe,

with propitious mind and rich abundance, to my
invocation inclined:

Mighty named, Imperial Artemis, born of Eubouleos
famed,

Be present, Goddess, to thy votaries kind, and give
abundance with benignant mind.

Tyche, you sit in Sophia's (*Wisdom's*) seat

bright light in darkness, you most excellent of gods

I seek by my own design to overcome a fence of other
design, I shall speak now of it with thy offering, those
things I shall do as well!

(*speak now of your desire and what you are doing to
appease the Goddess in your action*)

Daughter of Zeus Eleutherios,

Tykhe our ☐rakai goddess,

For your hand steers the ship of oceans on my flying
course,

and rules on land the march of savage wars,

So I shall achieve with thee, and Victory be mine!

APHRODITE / VENUS

Aphrodite, the Goddess of the Moon, she inspired love throughout the Hellenic world. Aphrodite is said to be close to Astarte, who later became Astaroth, the Crescent Horned Deity of heaven whom Sidonites worshipped. The name of Aphrodite soon overtook Astarte from the world of trade.

Aphrodite was born from sea form and had arisen from such primal origins, for her nature is as fluid as the depths of the sea. Upon rising up she emerged upon the island of Cythera and where she walked, beautiful flowers sprang up. The Gods were in awe of this, as she was most fair among all.

Aphrodite held the greatest powers of regeneration and the gift of life itself. She is the embodiment of the correspondence of desire and creation, not only from a nature manifestation yet also within humanity.

Aphrodite was said to have possessed a sacred girdle which inspired any near here, Hera also would "borrow" it when she wished to copulate with Zeus. The sacred plants and herbs to Aphrodite are myrtle, rose, apple and poppy among others.

Aphrodite seems to have originated from the Goddess Astarte, whom the Hebrews call Ashtoreth (*in demonology Astaroth, the fallen angel that inspires*). You may also conduct libation offerings to Aphrodite / Venus as one aspect of Lilith or the dark mother of Daimons, who inspires and is a beautiful example of love and lust perfected.

AN OFFERING TO APHRODITE

For Lust and the Love of Another

To the beautiful Aphrodite

Gold-crowned, luminous and dark

Whose dominion is the cities of all sea-set Kypros

The moist breath of Zephyros of western winds come

Over waves of the loud-moaning sea from the form in which you rise

May I gain victory in my conqest with my desired, ...name...

Of Kythereia, who of Kypros

Give unto me the kindly gift of your smile

Illuminate through me the brightness of your spirit

Hail, Goddess, Queen of Salamis

To Ourania, Illustrious, philommeideia Queen

Pontogenes, philopannyx of awful desire born

Who joins the world with harmony, from all lust brought

O Aphrodite, Grant my Desire!

ARES – MARS, the God of War. Notice the Dragon on the helmet, a symbol of war and conquering from times of antiquity. The later association of Mars with the Adversary Samael is found as being associated with the planet Mars, Samael being the "Angels of Poison" and who is a Seraphim.

ARES

Ares / Mars, the cruel and cunning god of war, battle and violence on the battlefield is one of the most aggressive of the gods. The son of Zeus and Hera, Ares is a manifestation of force applied and the determination of achieving victory. The interplay with Zeus and Ares is that he directs battles and Ares for the desire alone lusts through battle and especially the slaughter of man. Ares was known to send plagues and epidemics to those during times of strife; it made him on the edge of being a power of darkness. Ares / Mars continued to be a god of war and useful to the Olympian Gods.

Ares holds a powerful path in various cultures wherein the Greek religion spread in different manifestations. Herodotus wrote that the worship of Ares went on to Scythia where he was said to dwell, being a consistent war-focused culture, the Scythians worshipped Ares in the form of a sword and made sacrifices to him.

In the Luciferian tradition, Rome is the sacred city of Mars, the red planet whose angel is Samael the Adversary or Angel of Poison. While in a broader perspective, the Adversary may be viewed on a much deeper aspect as being a part of all the Gods and different aspects relating opposite conditions of mental perception.

The anthropomorphic imagery of Ares is as strong and violently interesting as the God's idea of spirit itself. It was written that he was insatiable in battle, blazing like the bright light of burning fire within his armor while standing in his chariot. Hesiod wrote that Ares was grim and whose chariot was driven by fleet-footed horses. Ares was blood covered and red as if eternally slaying men. His companions, Demois (fear) and Phobos (flight) empowered him to embody himself within the warring factions of the earth and grow stronger with their savagery.

Ares has no specific epithets of note, the imagery associated with Ares seems to be Roman or later. As mentioned, in Greek myth Ares is unpopular and violent, wherein Mars in his Roman manifestation was noble yet violent when need be.

Ares may be invoked in the sense of battle or strife, to overcome a challenge or meet a personal struggle in your life. Obviously you won't be going forth to fight with spear or sword for your challenges today, yet you must have the imagination to draw common associations and impart meaning with symbol with witchcraft and magick.

INVOCATION TO ARES THE WAR GOD

I invoke thee, blood covered one!

Ares, who exceeds in strength

Chariot-rider, harnessed in bronze, shield-bearer

Golden-helmed Ares who is mighty with spear

Hail thou spirit of strife and war!

Ares Mars, whirl your fiery spear and unite the planets

From sevenfold will they gather unto man

Ripping into the firmament of heaven

Assist me, empower me O lord of the crushing mace

Hail thou Prince of spilling blood!

Break down the laws of peace

Bring forth strife and the victory I desire!

Bring beside me the violent fiends of Death

To crush down the weakness in my soul!

Bless me Ares, Stand at my side to conquer my enemy!

Hail Ares!!!

Ares / Mars upon chariot riding off to battle

HERMES

Hermes is a powerful God who has knowledge on travel, diplomacy, language, writing, cunning intelligence, athleticism, astronomy and astrology. He was the messenger of Zeus, the King of the Gods.

Depicted as a bearded older man or youth, Hermes is shown carrying the wand or Caduceus which represents wisdom, winged boots representing speed and flight and often a winged travelers cap or chlamys cloak.

Hermes is the son of Zeus and Maia and was said to have been born in a cave. Hermes has knowledge of how to properly sacrifice to the Gods, to burn offerings and is credited with inventing numerous items. His power is found in his mind, for he is a gifted speaker and is patron guardian of diplomats.

Hermes uses the Caduceus, the Magickal staff which is said to open and close the eyes of mortals, obviously relating to initiation and the power of self-will. This staff was given to him by Apollo according to the Homeric hymn. The Romans knew Hermes as Mercury. His power in a left hand path perspective is speech and being able to communicate with cunning and purpose, not the mere speech of pointless conversation. Invoking Hermes and offering incense to him before travel, business meeting or interview would be a suitable foundation for working with Hermes.

Hermes like Zeus and the other gods has the ability to create and destroy as well. It was Hermes who slayed Argos, the watcher of Io who was the Sun-God. He had a single eye I his head which was the light of the sun and the body was covered in eyes. Hermes overmastered and in many ways devoured the Sun, thus shaping the light anew. Like a God of Light and Life, Hermes also was a God of Death in that he could drive the Sun away.

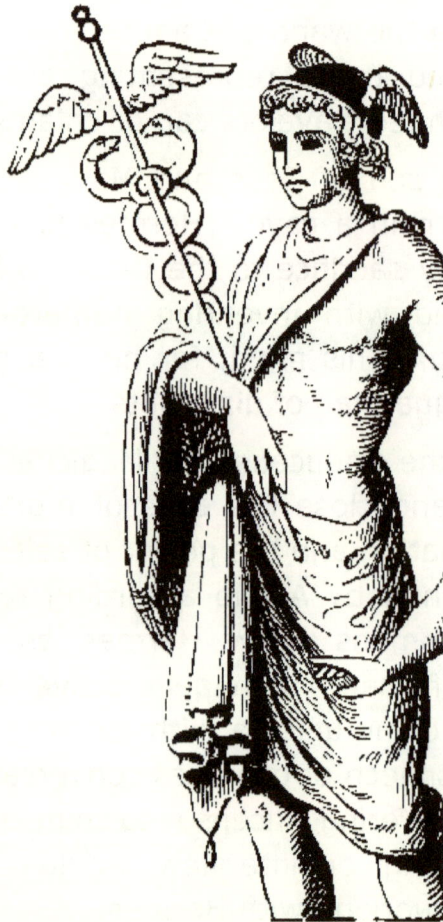

Hermes, associated by Luciferian Charles M. Pace to the Egyptian Hermanubis – Anubis, was the Son of Set and Isis. Hermes is the God of Magick along with Thoth.

INVOCATION OF HERMES

Unto the Messenger of the Gods and the Power of the Mind

I invoke thee Hermes

Son of Zeus and Maia, the Lord of Kyllene and Arkadia

Eriounes, Angelos Athanton

Whom Maia bare forth

Zeus affirmed Hermes over the Birds of Omen

And Grim-eyed lions, boars with cruel tusks

The Dogs who watch over flocks and the works of humanity

Hermes, who is the messenger of Hades

Whose power of the Dead and their path is great

For his power is initiation

Bless my purpose of ...statement of intent...

Hermes Khrysorrapis, Angelos Makaron

Bearer of the Khrysorrapis

Come and dwell in this house in friendship together

Who is abound with wisdom and strength

Hermes, come forth!

Athena Nikephoros (Athena bearing Victory)

ATHENA

Athena is a powerful Goddess who presides over War and strife; she asserts her destiny and position by all means necessary. Athena was a daughter of Zeus who was called the bright eyed one. The Libyan tradition mentions that Athena is the daughter of Poseidon and Tritonis. She was once mad at her father according to Herodotus and went to Zeus, who adopted her as his own daughter. Athena is the protector of agriculture and was credited as the inventor of the plough and rake. She brought the olive tree to the world and blessed the birth of horses.

The goddess appears throughout mythology as a Virgin Goddess, she stands between War and Peace, ensuring the careful balance of inner state and growth activities. Her war-desire is kept to a minimum, unlike Ares. She is said to be a Virgin Goddess, for she is safe from the desires and trappings of love.

Sacrifices were offered to Athena, Locrian maidens or children were offered to her every year and later on bulls were offered to her, earning the surname of Taurobolos.

Athena is depicted as wearing a helmet which is decorated with griffins, ram heads and sphinxes. She carries a Argolic shield which has a representation of Medusa within it. She often has a serpent with her, for it is sacred along with images of an owl, olive branch and spear. She is a strong female and does not show herself nude.

Offerings to Athena may be made with incense in honor of care and strength within the home, defense being a key focus point.

Athena from a Carthage Coin

OFFERING TO ATHENA

I call unto Athena, guardian of my sacred dwelling

I call to she who loves the deeds of war, the sack of cities and victory!

Hail Goddess, bring me good fortune and happiness!

Bring me the fortune of good defense of my dwelling and ensuring the protection of others in my home!

Hail to you, daughter of Zeus who holds the Aegis!

Athena who bears the immortal armor

flashed around the hovering lightning;

Fearful serpents breathed fire from her shield invincible

The crest of her great helmet swept the clouds

Accept my offering!

Demeter

DEMETER

Demeter is the powerful Olympian Goddess of Grain, Agriculture and the very substance of mankind. She is the mother of Persephone and reigns as a Queen of the Mystery cult of immortality. Demeter is the daughter of Cronus and Rhea, the sister of Hestia, Hades, Poseidon and Hera besides Zeus.

Demeter's myth centers around the association of health – both physical and mental and the initiatory struggle of both mother and father, those who seek to "find themselves". After Hades/Pluto took Persephone to the Underworld Demeter was stricken with grief. She wandered about in search for her daughter for nine days. Nine plays a significant initiatory key point from the cults of vampirism, Persian Yatukih associated with Druj Nasu and other magical systems from a left hand path perspective. Demeter met Hecate on the tenth day, asking if she had heard the cries of Persephone, yet still wondered who carried her away. Both Hecate and Demeter went to Helios, the Sun, who brought her the knowledge after the struggle of no bathing, nourishment or rest had established in days past. She learned that Hades carried her off, with the consent of Zeus.

Demeter was angry and would not return to Olympus for a time, dwelling among humans on earth. She gave presents and gifts to those who would receive her, although she cursed and punished those who did not. She went to Eleusis and brought famine to the earth.

Zeus had grown concerned over this affliction which could erase humanity and sent Iris to encourage

Demeter to return to Olympus. Zeus could not persuade her so he sent Hermes into Erebus to bring back Persephone. Hades or Aidoneus consented and gave Persephone a pomegranate to eat, that it would not inspire her to stay with Demeter. Hermes then borrowed the golden chariot of Hades to join her Mother.

Once in Eleusis Persephone was joined with Hecate. Demeter then did return to Olympus and granted that Persephone could spend part of the year in Erebus with Hades, enthroned in subterraneous darkness and this would be in the Winter.

The myth of Demeter relates to the initiation of the self into the mysteries of immortality, the nine represents struggle and the discovery of the True Will, Persephone (daughter) ascending from the Underworld represents the ascension of the Daimon or True Will coming forth as a Bringer of Light, descending back into Hades represents the knowledge continually gained from the shadow or subconscious. This path towards the immortality of the spirit is found in this careful balance.

Demeter may be offered to at several times during the course of the year, no matter which initiatory path you seek she may be thanked in accordance to the lessons she brings.

Antiochus IV Epiphanes struck a coin of Demeter veiled with an elephant on the back. The Goddess is most beautiful in that she offers the wisdom of foundation, desire and the loyalty of the True Will and self-discovery. Yellow and Green candles with white may be burnt in honor of Demeter.

A CALLING TO DEMETER

To Demeter Eleusinia

Universal, Beautiful Mother

I call unto thee, rich-haired Demeyer Semne Thea

In honor of your Trim-Ankled Persephone who Aidoneus enthroned

Bless is he among the men of the earth whom they freely love

Send forth Ploutos as Guest in our Great House

for Ploutos brings wealth to the bearer of Light

Hail the Queen of the land of Eleusis and sea-girt Paros

Agalaodoros

Horephoros, Anassa Deo

Be gracious unto me

Hail your beauteous daughter Persephone

Let my calls reach your glad heart and bestow your gifts upon me!

Demeter, whose head veiled and wearing a dark cloak

Guided through the underworld and through the Threshold

You bring knowledge and Will with heavenly radiance to all!

Deo Famed

August, thy Source of Wealth

All-Bounteous, Blessed and Divine

Goddess of Seed, of Fruits abundant

Who is fair, harvest and threshing in care!

Assessor of Great Bromios (Dionysos) who Bears Light

A chariot guided by Drakones is thine to guide

With orgies singing around thy throne

Hail thou loving, holy Koure

Bright Goddess Come!

Demeter with Serpent, the Goddess of the Earth and its bounty.

POSEIDON

The God of the Sea, the fluid element who is mighty and powerful. Poseidon is the Son of Cronus and Rhea and is the brother of Zeus, Hades, Hera and Demeter among others.

Poseidon is often depicted as a strong mature man who is bearded, sometimes half sea monster and other times a complete man. He is revered as the God of Water and the Ruler of the Sea, specifically the Mediterranean. He is able to call forth storms and great hurricanes, yet also has the power to grant successful voyages to those make offerings.

Poseidon bust from Nero coin

Poseidon holds a Trident which is a symbol of supreme power to him. He has the ability to shatter boulders and to summon forth storms. Herodotus writes that the worship of Poseidon was brought to the Greece from Libya and from a divinity from Pelasgian origins.

Poseidon has a palace beneath the depths of the sea close to Aegae in Euboea. He created horses and is a Patron god of charioteers. He has strong horses with golden manes and when he wishes he may ride forth in a chariot guided by horses over the sea. As he is the creator of Horses, he holds the epithets Hippios, Hippios Anax and even Equester.

Poseidon with Trident from Macedonian coin of siege expert Demetrios.

Monsters and Dragons of the Depths pay homage to him, respect him and often swim about him in joy. When he wishes, Poseidon may join the other Gods in Olympus yet prefers the ocean depths.

Poseidon upon chariot from ancient Greek design

The nature of Poseidon is never consistent; as his element is water his emotions are extreme and varying. His nature is like the sea, sometimes calm and soothing, sometimes violent and always changing.

Initiates may offer to Poseidon to establish knowledge of the subconscious mind and dreams to master emotions and further understand the self. In a literal perspective, you may offer to Poseidon near a great body of water or before travel over water.

INVOCATION OF POSEIDON

Hear me, Poseidon

Ruler of the Sea Profound

Who beneath the stormy chaos of the dark waters
beholds reign

Thy awful hand the brazen trident bears

All sound and calm to the Will of such Profound

I invoke thee, whose steeds the foam divides

Whose dark locks in which the waters glide

Thou great God who causes all monsters of the depths
to arise

Even trembling waves obey

Earth-covering, dark-haired God

Cerulean Daimon to catch glimpse

The monsters of the oceans ensorcel thee!

Bring forth wisdom and knowledge of my dreams

Abundance in tide and health beside

Poseidon, thou great god

Ennosigaios, Lord of Helikon and wide Aigai ascend!

God of the Depths Hear me!

With thy Trident ascend mastery over all water!

So it is done!

BA'AL BERIT

Ba'al Berit from coin of Antiochus IV Epiphanes

Ba'al Berit is a God associated with Berytus, a Phoenican colony which is near Beirut and Lebanon. This God, during the time of Antiochus IV Epiphanes, King of the Seleukid Empire assimilated the Greek Poseidon with Ba'al Berit to focus towards the Greek Religion. A specific coin was issued in this time with Ba'al Berit holding a Phiale or libation/offering bowl and a Trident in the Left Hand representing self-mastery and deification.

Having gained possession of a coin of Antiochus IV Epiphanes from between 175-164 BC, I conducted research, magical workings which led to this very book. Much of the history of Ba'al Berit is found previous before the Hebraic God.

Baalberith was present in Shechem in ancient Israel and was widely spread in the area. After the death of Gideon, many of the Jews worshipped Baalberith and is identical according to the Rabbis with Baal-zebub or "The Lord of Flies". At many points Baalberit was worshipped as a Fly as he was a symbol of the powers of Air, in addition to the Destructive Noon-Tide heat of the Sun. In addition the Sun holds as well the powers of creation; the fly brings the consumption of rotting meat and also is a curing factor of wounded areas of men and women.

It is written in the Jewish Encyclopedia that many Jews carried symbols of Baalberit and would kiss it in homage at certain times. While in later times Ba'al Berit was assimilated to Poseidon, his power of divinity grew. Initiates seeking the wisdom of old may seek Ba'al Berit as the God of Magickians, the Wisdom of Old and that of the subconscious mind. You may utilize any items deemed necessary towards the act including flies or symbols of Poseidon depending on type of working.

Beelzebub from Camlet as Lord of Flies

THE RITE OF BA'AL BERIT

To invoke the Ancient Essence of Power

Hail thou, Ba'al of Flies

Who resides in lofty heights by the powers of Air

I invoke thee Ba'al Berit who brings wisdom to the seeking

I invoke thee Ba'al Berit who brings power to the strong and wise

By the powers of the Sea, Hail thou God of the Depths

Whose cult was revered ages ago

Who was the God of those Wise ones who reject the Sheepherding God

Highest of the Gods, Lord of the Sea

Ba'al Berit of the Golden Trident

Surrounded by the theres in a ring swim around

Encircled by Drakones primal

Hail Thou Ba'al Berit!

I invoke thee Golden Power of the Sun

In Destruction and Creation!

Empower me with thy spirit; lend to me your Trident!

Baal as the Sun God

BA'AL

Baal and Ba'al Hammon is the Phoenican God of Tyre and Carthage. Baal-Hadad is the Syrian god of storms and the wind, his name meaning 'Lord of Thunder". As the "cloud-rider" he was associated with Zeus in other comparative myths.

Ba'al-Hammon is known from the settlement of Zindsirli and is associated with the Phoenican settlement. The Carthage Supreme God was revered as a God of Fertility and is associated with Ammon, an Oasis God. Often the Romans identified Ba'al-Hammon with Kronos or Saturnus.

Ba'al-Qarnain means "Lord of Two Horns" is a Punic God who has two mountains peaks associated with him near the gulf of Tunis. He is sometimes called Saturnus Balcarnensis. The Two Horned one is a title Alexander the Great gained after conquering his empire. His portrait is shown on several ancient coins with the Horns of a Ram which refers to Power over the Earth. The initiatory understanding in this aspect is that by Will alone did he conquer and command the world around him.

The title associated with Ba'al-Qarnain, "Dhulqarnen" is from a Berber sect of witch practitioners who light fires and dance in religious ecstasy, the world "Dhulqarnen" means "two-horned" one and "Lord of Two Centuries" according to Idries Shah.

Ba'al-Sarnrnin is the "Lord of Heaven" and was worshipped in ancient Syria, Mesopotamia, Carthage and Cypress. On a Seleucid Empire coin Ba'al Sarnrnin is shown bearing a half-moon on his brow and carrying in one hand a Sun with Seven Rays.

Among the Phoenican people, Baal-bek was the Sun God, who may be the same as Helios as the Greek manifestation of the Solar God. The ancient city of Tyre was dedicated to Baal-bek as well as Tarsus. He was a generative and lofty God, whose symbols were grapes and bulls. Just as Baal Berit draws close association, the God of the Sun held both a creative and destructive aspect. Baal in Phoenican culture represented the generative principle associated with nature, while Tanit or Ashtoreth represented the receptive and generative principle.

There are many legends associated with Baal and the balanced nature in which he commands his will upon the earth. One specific legend is that of Baal and the Prince of the Sea called Yamm. Building a great house for Baal, Yamm sought the assistance of the God Kathar. Kathar represents the wonders of beyond the sea or the area in which people dwelt. The God Kathar dwelt in Crete, yet his patrimony was Egypt.

Kathar soon felt he needed offerings and Baal resisted. The Goddess Anat, who is the sister of Baal is quite warlike in nature.

Armed with clubs, YAGRUSH and AYMUR "fly to Baals hand like eagles" and in battle Kathar's head. Astarte proclaims Baal as King and Yamm dead. It is suggested that Yamm represented the sea people who terrorized the coats during a period of antiquity.

Upon this victory, Anat is fighting with combatants in the Palace of Baal. Anat is described as massacring warriors and up to her knees in blood, she has a pile of heads from those she kills. Anath (an alternative spelling) also decorates herself in the heads of those she takes in battle, much like KALI, her Indian manifestation.

Baal also has brothers and Anat is the sister of the Prince of the Sea, Tannin and Loran, the torturous serpent and the beast with seven heads. Here we can see some esoteric relation to some later apocalyptic considerations of these powers.

Baal also brought order by defeating and subduing Lotan, the Hebraic Leviathan who is a seven headed dragon.

Offerings to Baal depending on purpose may be done with incense accordingly.

Baal holding the weapons of War with horned helmet.

Baal Hammon with Goat herd and horned

Tanit from a Carthage coin

TANIT

Tanit-baal is the supreme Goddess of Carthage and whose epithet is PENE BAAL meaning "Face of Baal". Being the Queen of Heaven, mother and Goddess and symbols of her worship is the pomegranate, wheat the dove. The symbol of Tanit is a triangle with horizontal beams on it. She held a relation to the Moon much in a similar way as Diana, Hecate and Artemis. The primary symbol of Tanit interestingly enough was a trapezoid

Tanith or Tanit had a lunar quality and was highly powerful among the Carthaginian people. Apulueius describes Tanit as the mistress of the elements, the highest of deities and the Queen of the Manes.

Tanit was described as riding upon a Lion and thus holds a powerful and fierce nature. Tanit is considered a heavenly Goddess of War, in Egyptian her name being Neith (nit) which is a War Goddess.

Tanit is said to have her origins in Ugarit, a small colony around Sidon or Tyre. The name Tanit comes from the violent bride of Baal, Anat. In the Ugaritic Ba'al Hadad cycle Anat is a fierce war goddess, whose appearance in the Ras Shamra describes Anat appearing as a furious warrior in battle, wading knee-deep in blood, severing heads, cutting off hands and binding the heads to her torso (like Kali) and keeping the hands. When she was killing and driving off townsfolk with arrows she was filled with joy. Anat was also a consumer of flesh and blood, providing a balance to her appearance as a Goddess of Heaven.

ASHTORETH-KARNAIM

Astoreth holds close association to Astarte and Astaroth, the Goetic demon of inspiration who according to some demonologists and Luciferians is a God taking many deific masks. Ashtoreth-Karnaim or Karnain is the Goddess of Heaven, the Astarte of Two Horns thus her symbol is a crescent horn. She appears as a naked female, sometimes sitting upon a throne or having a dove sitting on her hand. It is said that Ashtoreth is the same as Tanith once worship spread through the Mediterranean. She is connected also with Ishtar the Goddess of Love as well.

Astoreth

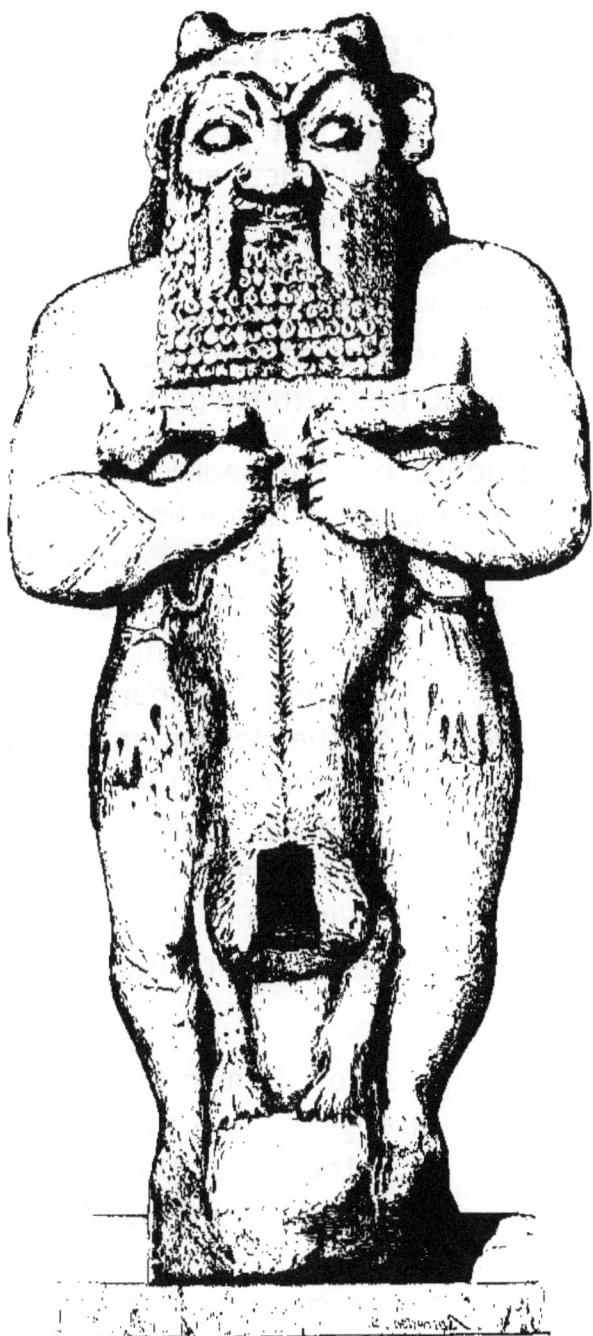

Melkart / Herakles

MELQART – HERAKLES

The patron God of the ancient city of Tyre, Melqart/Baal Tsur is called "The Fire of Heaven" and is partially an underworld God and son of Ba'al Hammon. It is commonly suggested that Melqart is one of the ancient forms of Herakles, as Meqart was a God who dies and is reborn along with vegetation. Ba'l Sur is "Lord of Tye" and is a name associated with Melqart.

Melqart was said to have appeared to Hannibal in a dream before he took to fighting Rome. In this dream it was said Hannibal saw a serpent crashing though the forest and causing wide spread destruction where it went, claps of thunder and lightning flashes were gathering behind the serpent. Melqart spoke to him "what thou beholdest is the desolation of Italy, follow thy star and inquire no further into the dark counsels of heaven". This very record was written by the Roman historian Livy. Such would be an example of the Deific Mask communicating with the subconscious mind, something like the Holy Guardian Angel or Daimon of man.

Melqart holds similar association to the Greek Herakles in that he is willed-strength, overcoming and mastering problems and a God of the Vegetation cycle. Melqart's time of worship was based around 1200 BC to about 200 BC although seems to have survived a bit longer. In Tyre, Melqart was the consort of Astarte and Tanith and seems to have been adapted from Nergal, the Babylonian God of War and the Underworld.

Another perhaps more correct spelling of Melqart is "Milk-Qart" which is "King of the City" and Melkart, while Milqartu was the Phoenician God of Tyre from Akkadian origins.

Melkarth as a word is said to have come from Melek and Kartha which means "king of the city" and related him in many aspects to the Greek Herakles. One of the physical forms of Melkarth is that he appears as a muscular man adorned in a lion's skin and holding a club.

Mithridates VI Dionysos bust as Herakles. Mithridates was the King of Pontus and a formidable enemy of Rome, winning many battles.

OFFERING CALL TO BA'AL & TANITH

I offer libations to thee

Sacred incense to thee

To the great Goddess Tanith

To our Lord and Powerful God-Spirit Baal-Hammon

I offer to thee, for I am ...name...

That I may achieve the victory of which I speak *...insert desire...*

So it shall be!

HEPHAESTUS

Hephaestus is the God of Fire, the same as Vulcan of the Roman religion. Hephaestus is the son of Zeus and Hera. Being the God relating to Volcano eruptions, his power of fire and the forge is foreseen as a God of Great Works and the process of the forge. Some Luciferians or Left Hand Path practitioners may view Hephaestus as the Grecian manifestation of the Semitic Tubal-Cain. Hephaestus built his own palace which was imperishable and shined brightly like the stars. His strike of the anvil begot weapons and great armor, for his workmanship was legendary. The cyclopes, Steropes and Pyracmon are his workmen.

Hephaestus, like Athena brings skills to humanity in which they may defend themselves and make weapons and great instruments of war when needed.

INVOCATION TO HEPHAESTUS

For Works of Change and Improvement

I invoke the Hephaestus, from your Bright Starlike Palace

Who gave unto Phoibos Apollon the Mist about his shoulders

Who carried a terrible Aegis, whom you as Khalkeus

Gave to Zeus to wear the Terror of Mortals

Hephaestus, God of Fire and the Forge of Strength

I command thy power through me to move towards my goals!

Who gave unto Athene the Aegis she wears in angry moods

Whose surface of gold is like scaly serpent-skin

Gorgon herself residing upon Athena's breast

Whose eyes ever watchful

That by your Forge shall I be given the gifts which shall empower me

By my own desire and Will

For I am God Manifest!

Hail to you Hephaestus, God of Fire and Strength!

ZALMOXIS

Zalmoxis is a man who became a God to the Getae-Scythians who was considered immortal. Herodotus wrote that he was told by the Pontic Greeks that Zalmoxis was a man who was a disciple of Pythagoras who then traveled in many places with much knowledge and wealth acquired. Herodotus wrote at one point Zalmoxis went on a journey to Egypt and gained initiatory knowledge of the immortality of the spirit, where they could pass death and gained spiritual existence entirely. Zalmoxis was said to have then went to the mountain of Kogaion and went to Hades to live for three years, in the forth returning to the joy of the Getae-Dacians and Scythians.

Zalmoxis according to Plato had skill with incantation and many considered him the same as Sabazius. What is clear from a left hand path perspective is that Zalmoxis is a God of Magickians or Luciferians, he embodies the antinomian spirit of self-liberation and self-deification by focused initiation. When the path grows boring, results lack or unfruitful Zalmoxis represents the determination to continue and see past the test.

ARTEMIS

The Olympian twin spirit of Apollo, Artemis is a virginal spirit who protects the girl up to the date of marriage. She holds a hunting bow and short chiton (a type of dress). Artemis is a Goddess of hunting, wild animals and is equal with Apollo in causing sudden death and disease, using also her arrows and with Apollo targets women and girls. Her epithets in this form is THEA APOLLOUSA. Artmetis is derived ancient Greek times, meaning "Uninjured" and "healthy" and represents her spiritual and physical purity. She also may avert sickness and death, her epithets is then THEA SOTERIA. Fathers and mothers may encourage a young girl to focus on Artemis and what they find about her within them, the strength of an individual mind that does not fall prey to early sexual relations of a young teen if they so desire. Another epithets of Artemis as the protectress of the young is paidotrophos. As Goddess of the hunt, she love the rush of the chase and hunt, for amoung the immortals she is the huntress. This goddess from the Brauronian Attica is specifically violent; boys were scoured at her altar until they dripped blood near or on her altar. Taurians sacrificed strangers to her for a time.

She held many powers, strangely other than causing plague had little in common with Apollo.

Artemis may be offered to by giving a bowl of honey with rose *water.* The following invocation is adapted from the Homeric Hymn 9 to Artemis.

Artemis

CALLING TO ARTEMIS

"I call unto Artemis, thou virginal sister of Hekatos (the far-shooter),

Parthenos Iokheaira (the virgin who delights in arrows), who was fostered with Apollon.

She waters her horses from Meles deep in reeds (a river in Lydia), and swifty drives her all-golden chariot through Smyrna to vine-clad Klaros where Apollon Argyrotoxos (god of the silver bow), sits waiting for Hekatebolon Iokheaira (far-shooting delighter in arrows).

Hail to you, Artemis, in my calling and to bless my work as well. I call unto you to work through me with (name goal, protection or focus attributed).

I call to you, Artemis Khryselakatos (with shafts are of gold),

Keladeine (strong-voiced),

Parthenon Aidoine (the revered virgin),

Elaphebolos (dear-shooting),

Iokheaira (delighter in arrows), own sister to Apollon Khrysaor (of the golden sword).

Over the shadowy hills and windy peaks she draws her golden bow, rejoicing in the chase, and sends out grievous shafts.

Hail to you, Theroskopos Iokheaira (the huntress who delights in arrows) slackens her supple bow and goes to the great house of her dear brother Phoibos Apollon, to the rich land of Delphoi, there to order the lovely dance of the Mousai whose songs are delightful Hail to you, children of Zeus and Leto!

I give to you Goddess…..(incense burnt, offering left).

So you shall open your eyes unto me and look favorably upon my offering!

Nike, Goddess of Victory

NIKE

Nike is the winged Daimon of victory, in war and in daily life. Nike was brought forth by her mother Styx, the Goddess of the Underworld River Styx. Styx is the personified Daimon of Stygos, or Hatred. Styx gave Zeus four of her offspring to guard his throne and ascend his power. They are Zelos(Rivalry), Bia(Force) Kratos (Strength) and Nike (Victory). Nike was appointed the Charioteer of Zeus which led him to Victory to become King of Olympios and the Gods, from a left hand path or Luciferian perspective this was his "crossing of the abyss" or initiatory struggle for self-deification. When Typhon laid siege to Olympios, it was Nike who was the only left besides Zeus, as she was loyal to the higher aspect of the Daimon, the aspiration of the intellect and the illuminated manifestation. Typhon, being the force of primal change which could not be destroyed, only mastered and used as a power of change as Zeus willed it.

To have a symbol or statue of Nike is to recognize the consistency of Willpower and the determination which leads to victory, thus having a small image/statue of Nike within your home is a reminder that by Will and Belief you will be victorious in your actions.

PAN

The god of the mountain wilds and the green areas of the Earth, Pan first was thought to wander the hills of Arkadia playing his pan-pipes. His image is one of joy, please and wisdom, for his presence alone aroused Panic when through the Wilds.

Being a lover of Nymphs, Pan is often decipted as half-goat and man who is perpetually aroused, seeking a companion. In Luciferian and Left Hand Path circles, Pan is accepted within the Qabala context of Aleister Crowley's numerical equivalent 77, being Night and Death, Sexual Creation and the force which inspires life.

A friend of Dionysos, Pan is a word associated with the rustic term meaning "all". One of the symbols of Pan is the phallic symbol representing fertility and the grape vines of Dionysos.

The Goddess Anahita

ANAHITA

The Goddess Anahita is the divinity of the Waters, the manifestation of fetility, healing and wisdom. She was revered in the Avestan texts of Zoroaster, being a Goddess whose power nurtures crops and herds. Ardwisur Anāhīd is the name of the Goddess from the Middle Persian and Sassanian texts. She is the lady of wild beasts, passionate, powerful and wild. Anahita is said to ride upon a chariot drawn by four horses named "wind", "clouds", "rain" and "sleet" and is adorned in a golden embroidered robe, a crown, necklace and earrings, a golden breast ornament and resides in stately places.

Anahita, being a Persian Goddess was powerful from the times of the Parthians to the Sassanians until the coming of Islam. The Zoroastrian pantheon allowed this powerful manifestation of water and fertility to maintain her divinity.

Azhi Dahaka, the storm-druj of Ahriman, who according to myth ruled ancient Persia for a thousand years offered sacrifice to Anahita as well.

'To her did Azi Dahaka, the three-mouthed, offer up a sacrifice in the land of Bawri, with a hundred male horses, a thousand oxen, and ten thousand lambs. 'He begged of her a boon, saying: "Grant me this boon, O good, most beneficent Ardvi Sura Anahita! That I may make all the seven Karshvares of the earth empty of men" – Avesta

HELIOS

Helios is the Greek guardian of oaths and a God of Sight. He dwelt in a golden, beautiful palace within the river Okeanos. He would emerge from those depths at dawn driving a chariot drawn by four, fiery winged horses and was crowned in the aura of the Sun. It was said he would reach the land of the Hesperides in the Western Sky and would descend back to his abode.

Associated with the Light-Bringer Apollon, the Vulcan/Hephaistos, Helios provides, along with Apollo a fantastic foundation for the symbolism commonly associated with Luciferian symbolism. Helios was a God adopted by Nero Caesar as was Apollo as the player of the lyre. Helios was depicted in art as a handsome, beardless younger man clothed in purple robes and had an Aura-Crown of the Sun. His chariot was as bright as the Sun for he, like Apollo brought Light. Once he hit the Western sky the shadow of Helios was like "Noctifer", or "Nightbringer".

Homer described Helios as giving Light to Men and the Gods. This may be considered as "wisdom" and such associations/offerings be made unto Helios-Apollo just as Nero Caesar may have done as being an embodiment of Light. Helios rises in the East and his greatest strength is Noon.

Descending in the darkness of the West, he returned to the depths of Oceanus wherein he would rise again at Dawn. Hyperion and Theia became lovers and joined to beget Helios (Sun), Selene (Moon) and Eos (dawn) for which all the Gods lived under.

Invocations and Offerings to Helios may be done either at Dawn or at Noon-time, when Helios has the greatest power. You may envision him similar to the Sun Card of Aleister Crowley's "Thoth Deck" or the Lucifer of the Sun card in the "Luciferian Tarot", both provide meaningful imagery.

Helios, the God of the Sun who is often identified with Apollo. Nero Caesar held close association with Helios/Apollo.

INVOCATION TO HELIOS

AGIOS O HELIOS

Helios, crown of the Sun

Who shines upon humanity and the Immortal Gods

Whose piercing gaze sends light with his eyes

Gazing triumphantly with his Golden Helmet

I call to thee Helios, Empower me with Wisdom and Strength!

Helios, whose Bright rays shine dazzlingly from the Aura

Whose bright locks extend the power of majesty

Who is the Archon which brings awakening to all

I invoke thee and offer to thee

Who guides the Golden, fiery chariot each Dawn

Whose purple, rich garment flutters against the chaos of the sky

Phoebus, Light of the Morning

Who wears the Corselet Woven of Twelve Stars

Lend to me thy Diadem of Myriad Rays!

Place your Golden Helmet of the Sun

Awaken and Crown me with your Fire Helios!

Who shall wind me with the Seven Rays upon my hair

In white adorned great conqueror!

Lend to me thy Fiery Robe that I may Guide your Golden Chariot!

I offer to thee Helios!

All-seeing, All-hearing!

O thou Helios, if I go far over the earth then Illuminate me!
So it done!

Eosphoros – the Morning Star

EOSPHOROS – The Morning Star

Eosphoros, called EOS which is the Latin Aurora, the Goddess of the Morning Red who brings the Light of Day from the East, the sister of Helios. Eosphoros means "Dawn Bringer". This title, when combine with Zeus, Apollo, Helios, Mars, Hades and Typhon creates the Medieval Lucifer from symbolism as being "the devil" yet holds a deeper symbolism of self-creation and antinomian self-deification.

It was the duty of Eos at the close of night to ride on her chariot driven by the horses Phaeton and Lampus to announce the coming of morning to the Gods and Humanity.

Eosphorus may be viewed as the Luciferian Goddess of self-inspiration and direction, the freedom by wisdom and knowledge from the God of Slaves and sheepherding promises.

Offerings to Eosphorus may be pure invocations and callings to wisdom and the freedom from restrictive belief. Burn frankincense and face the coming of the Dawn. You may visualize Lucifer as the Bringer of Light as the traditional male-Archon or simply the Goddess in this form of Light.

INVOCATION OF EOSPHORUS

AGIOS O EOSPHORUS

I invoke thee O Illuminated Eosphorus!

O thou Goddess Eos, who draws close to Olympos!

Who bears the message of the Light of Zeus & Immortals!

Yellow-robed Goddess who brings early light over the earth!

Whose carries this Fire to immortals alike!

We dwell in the ecstasy of night

Awaiting Erigeneia awaiting Ethereal Dawn

The brightest of Stars, called Eosphoros!

Who is Adversarial as ORTHRIA

The most lofty of heralds in the light of early-rising Dawn

Called Eos Erigineia, Light Bringing Power of the Sun!

With thy steeds of flight, gather Lampos and Phaithon!

The light of all-seeing Eos the Dawn ASCEND!

Eosphoros, Lovely Light of the Immortal Aous!

White Horsed powers bring the light from within me!

That I shall bear the Sun as the Radiant Crown!

With your bright eyes who beholds the towering crags of Pelion!

It is your hour of morning in which you illuminate the Eastern Sky!

Ascend through me, Come Forth CHRYSOPACHUS!

Come Lucifer, Come Eosphoros wake Aurora and the Chariot of Day!

Rise with dewy hair, illuminating the Sky Red!

May Night Sleep again, to rise as Noctifer!

LUCIFER HAS RISEN, FORERUNNER OF THE DAWN!

Until Hesperos is kindling his evening rays!

Unto Thee O Noble Lucifer,

Aurora rising from Mygdonian resting-place

Who calls down the shadows, CROCOPEPLOS

Through the clouds crimson Lucifer turns his late fires

With a slow steed leaves an world until the Fiery Father Helios

Is replenished, Hail Eosphorus!

Phosphorus – Hesperos and Eos

HESPEROS – THE NIGHT BRINGER

Like Eosophoros, Hesperos is one of the Gods of the Star Venus. Hesperos is Phorphorus/Phaesphoros which is Lucifer, the bringer of light associated with the planet Venus. This same planet is called Hesperus which is Vesper, Noctif or Nocturnus. Luciferians call this "Noctifer" for "nightbringer" when referring to the dark or shadow aspect, Phosphorus, Eosophoros being "Lucifer" for the "Lightbringer". In Greek mythology, Phosphorus as a personification is a son of Astaeus and Eos and the father of Ceyx and Daedalion. Phosphorus is used widely in mythology relating as a surname of Goddess of Light and the Moon, being Artemis / Diana Lucifera as well as Hecate (Eurip. Helen 569) as She is the Goddess which "carries the torch". Over a period of time the two, Lucifer and Noctifer was combined into two Gods – essentially a form of the Adversary without any specific 'violent' or 'demonic' attributions. One may perceive the Two Eosphoros and Hesperos as being two specific brain associations, governed by night and day. Moods and inspirations brought to a sense of clarity and perception.

Diosdorus wrote that he was worshipped with divine honors and was regarded as the fairest star in the heavens. In Roman mythology Lucifer is designated as both Hesperus/Noctifer and Eosphoros/Lucifer.

PROMETHEUS

One of the associated gods of the concepts of Lucifer, Prometheus stands as one aspect of this process. The name "Prometheus" is one which signifies "forethought" and relates to the fire which he took to humanity. Prometheus is an immortal god, who brought the Fire of Consciousness to humanity. Prometheus is a Titan yet was overcome by Zeus, who kept a tight leash on his reigns of humanity – differently than the Judeo-Christian God.

Like the Watchers or Grigori, Prometheus gave humanity the gift of fire, mathematics, astronomy and the art of writing – so very close to the Watchers in their purpose with humanity.

KYBELE / CYBELE

Cybele was the Phyrgian "Matar Kubileya/Kubeleya "Kubeleyan Mother", which means "Mountain Mother" and relates to her power as the origins of the wild earth manifest. Cybele is a Goddess of Earth from a more predatory, dark yet not quite "demonic" aspect. Lions are under her sway, the wilds of the mountains are under her command.

Cybele is one of the earliest Goddesses, first thought to have taken hold in Anatolia between 7,000 B.C. her power as "Mistress of the Animals" grants her similar association to the Sumerian-Chaldean LILITH as holding power over Lions. Cybele found her home in the Roman Empire.

Kybele was connected with Hecate, Rhea, Demeter and she was known to have priests who have castrated themselves in her honor and dress as women. During the plague of Athens in 430 B.C. a temple to Cybele was built to honor the Goddess.

Like Hecate, the Cult of Cybele often was considered similar in aims. An older dedication stone of Hecate shows a crescent moon and females dedicated to Hecate wearing what is called a Polis, a crown worn by Cybele.

Cybele upon her chariot drawn by lions

The Potnia therion or "mistress of animals" is a powerful foundation for the understanding of the goddess in a balanced perspective. Rhea or Cybele is the Bride of Cronus or Time, the father of Zeus.

Invoking and offering to Rhea-Cybele is done for the insight of animals, understanding feminine spiritual needs and balancing motherhood with everyday life.

INVOCATION OF KYBELE – RHEA

I invoke thee, Illustrious Kybele-Rhea

To the Mother of the beasts of the world

With thy Chariot drawn by fierce lions, terrible and strong

Mother of Zeus, whose arm may wield the avenging lightning bolt

And shake the foundations of the world

Whose spirit finds joy in mountains and tumultuous fight

Humanity's howlings being a part of your sacred music

Bride of Kronus who is the Mother of the Gods

Come, Blessed Mother of Therionick Powers

To Meter Therion, All beautiful and powerful

Come, mighty power, propitious to our rites,

All-taming, blessed, Phrygian Protectress,

Come, Kronos' great queen,

Rejoicing in the drums of Black Night and Burning Day!

SELENE

Titan Goddess of the Moon. Selene is called also Mene or from the latin "Luna" and is depicted as a Goddess riding a chariot guided by winged horses. Her symbol is a crescent upward with regards to bull horns as well. Selene is considered the daughter of Hyperion and Theia and is a sister of Helios and Eos. Some consider Selene a daughter of Zeus and Pallas. The love of Selene was a prince named Endymion who was given eternal youth and immortality by Zeus. He awakens at night to go forth with the heavenly bride at night. Selene is shown on the pedestal of the throne of Zeus at Olympia riding a horse. Elis holds a statue of her with two Horns.

Offerings made to Mene or Selene may be done with the symbol of a crescent moon, calling forth the powers of intuition and instinctual knowledge, a symbol Luciferians identify with Hecate and Lilith in their maiden or Goddess form. If one wishes to invoke Selene for the desires of the heart, do so with the Moonstone, for it is said to be empowered and sacred unto Selene. For further workings and comparisons on Luciferian methods of sorcerous calls, Selene is found in the HECATE area and with Artemis as the Triad of Goddess.

CALLING DOWN THE MOON GODDESS SELENE

I invoke thee, call thee from the Blue-black vault of Stars!

Thea Basileia, Hear my calls!

I call down by the powers of the Moon

O thou long-winged Selene

Whose immortal head is crowned a radiance descended from heaven

Falling to embrace earth O pale, haunting face

Whose beauty arises from such shining light

Mene, Goddess who is illuminated with the light of golden crown

Whose body bathed in the waters of Okeanos

Whose steed of night guides you across the sky

Descend into me and inspire my visions O Goddess!

Who sends forth diffusing silver light, bull-horned Goddess

Whose beauty captures the spirit of all

Or enthrones them in their own light

Who wonders through the gloom of night

Stars surrounded, holding the torch of light

Splendid Queen of Night

Shine upon and through me thy Blessed, prosperous rays

Hail to you Goddess Selene, my offerings to you!

With my rope of night and desire

I call you down Goddess of Fresh Blood

Horned and entreating

I command the Moon to empower me

In the name of the Goddess, Heavenly and Horned in Bestial Light

Allow your light to shine with me as the serpent of wisdom

In the night when I free my spirit in the dreaming world

Let me enter the Great Sea with Knowledge of the Primal

If I wish to go forth on the air of night

Grant me the power of flight

Hail to thee Selene, Goddess of the Horned Moon

Serpent splendor

Who is most noble of night

Exalted empress and queen of shadows cloak

Held high by lofty illustrious moon

So it shall be!

BENDIS

A Thracian Goddess of the Moon, Bendis is depicted as wearing a Thracian body-suit, a tight fitting garment with an animal skin cap. She holds in her hands a spear and a drinking bowl. Plato wrote of Bendis and her rites as being sometimes held on horseback and by carrying a torch, quite similar to Hekate. Specific reference by Hesychius informs us that Bendis is often called 'dilonchos', as she held a duty towards the heavens or empyrean and one on earth. She had two lights, her own and one obtained from the sun.

Kybele

ISHTAR & INANNA

Ishtar is the Babylon Goddess of fertility, war and sex. Essentially, she is the manifestation of Lilith or the Daemonic Feminine within a socially mainstream aspect in ancient Babylonia. While Lilith and her brood were feared and respected, Ishtar was more accepted as a Goddess representing elements that cultures could embrace more readily.

Ishtar is the manifestation of Venus within the Babylonian pantheon, Erech was her holy city and she presided over sacred prostitution. Ishtar has a specifically deadly quality to her love, many of her lovers were killed by her embraces – which draws another association to Lilith as the Goddess of Vampires and night phantoms.

Ishtar and Inanna are very much like Ereshkigal, the Queen of the Underworld although they meet in various aspects in the myths of old. Ishtar and Ereshkigal, like Typhon and Zeus, are very close and related in nature, while opposite, may be viewed in association of similar initiatory properties.

Inanna is the Goddess of the Morning and Evening Star as well, a hymn from the time of Iddin-Dagan of Isin gives praise to her as she rises in the sky in the evening. At the time of each New Moon she gives council to the other gods. She rejoices in war and bloodlust.

In the morning hour, she is the Goddess which wakes both man and beast. Offerings may be made to Inanna as the Goddess of the Morning and Evening Stars, essentially the aspect of Lilith as beautiful Goddess. She is horned and cruel when needed, yet her embrace brings death to some.

Inanna is also the Goddess of Prostitution, she offers protection to harlots and her association is found with the Evening Star in this aspect.

In Thelema and Typhonian Magick, Inanna and Lilith are indeed the faces or masks of Babalon, the Great Crimson Harlot. She is a force a viable initiation.

Ishtar is also the Goddess of War, her name is also associated with Astarte who like Ishtar, is a Goddess of Love and the violence of War.

Inanna is also connected with the lighting of fires, for she is the "Lady of a myriad offices". She also puts out fires and causes death.

One thing Inanna is never viewed as a mother or helpmate, she is the viable Adversary in the form of Goddess, she is both beautiful and bestial, like Lilith.

Those witches or pagans who seek Inanna will no doubt find the initiatory similarities and avenues of Lilith and Inanna, something which has been strived for in modern left hand path practice. The Goddess is both destructive and creative in all, the dark or violent aspect is not destructive as well.

HYMN TO INANNA

Hail thou Great Goddess of Heaven

The One who has many faces and masks

Hail thou Queen of Heaven

Illuminating and brilliant

I invoke thee Inanna

Who is the torch which flares in the sky

Thou heavenly light, shining bright within

Thou great queen of Heaven, Inanna Hail!

Thou Queen of the Anunnaki

Who is crowned and illuminated with Horns

Oldest daughter of Suen

Inanna, we call to thee!

Beautiful majesty, Goddess of War and Lust!

Who comes forth in evening

As a brightly burning torch

Who is Great in her power

Like the Sun and the Moon

Of your greatness I offer thee Praise

Rise up through me, Hail thou Inanna!

Inanna – Ishtar

Who can break down the doors of the dead!

She who can cause the dead to rise and devour

The living!

Hail thou, beautiful and terrible one!

Ishtar – Inanna, the Goddess of War. The Goddess is shown with elements very close to Lilith. Her symbol is also the 8 pointed star.

IV. ΘΕΟΙ ΚΗΤΗΟΝΙΟΙ

DARK GODS AND THE UNDERWORLD

Satan as Zeus offering the Judeo-Christian Nazerene dominion over the earth from old Christian illustration.

ZEUS LYKAIOS

The God of Heaven known as Zeus also held specific balance as both a light and dark god. Zeus Lykaios dwelled in the mountains and held a hidden place surrounded with the cruel aspects of nature.

It is Zeus Lykaios whom embodied the destructive and violent aspects of nature in the incarnation of a ravening wolf. Many would offer human sacrifice to Zeus Lykaios, to appease nature itself in the lonely places of his sacred abode. It is also lore that in Arcadian Highlands, where Zeus Lykaios was worshipped, that if one who tasted the flesh of the sacrifice victim, would change for nine years into a werewolf, wandering the desolate land and seeking the flesh of others.

The werewolf must be seen as a power of the subconscious; the primal more animalistic side unleashed or brought to the surface. When people attempt to hide their dark instincts or desires, they later make themselves known in bad and unwanted ways. The werewolf is a mental process alone.

Zeus Maimaktes the Serpent God

ZEUS MEILICHIOS – MAIMAKTES

A name meaning "Easy-to-be-entreated", this epithet is for Zeus in an obscure chthonic daimon form, who also carried the name of Maimaktes which means "raging" and assumes the nature of "thirsting for blood". Zeus Meilichios demands holocausts, would seek to devour the entire victim. His power dreadful, his nature as predatory and fierce as Typhon. The author of "Prolegomena to the study of Greek Religion" by Jane Ellen Harrison wrote of visiting a sanctuary dedicated to the Meilichians at Myonia in Locris, which was a grove with an altar. Sacrifices were made to "the Melichians" and nighttime and it was customary to consume the flesh before the sun rises. Zeus Meilichios seems to have overmastered the Melichians and become the divinity in which to offered to, as his form was horrid and terror-inspiring.

Zeus Seraphs as Bearer of Black Flame

Zeus Meilichios, like Hades, was associated with wealth, thus a large number of pigs were sacrificed to Zeus Meilichios. Meilichios was considered by "Easy-to-be-entreated", thus the name meaning gracious, yet held a mask of Maimaktes, "he who rages eager, panting and thirsting for blood". Maimaktes-Meilichios is described by Harrison as being a double headed god, thus he was an early manifestation of balance, of both darkness and light, The Adversary. Zeus at one point in the fifth century B.C. was considered an early monotheistic deity, although he held many attributes and even had the aspect of Zeus-Hades as the lord of the underworld as well.

There are two reliefs found at the Peiraeus sanctuary that at the time of 1903 at the Berlin museum, one is Zeus Meilichios which is dedicated to him, inscribed below a coiled beast-serpent. One of the first and only images of Zeus as a Typhonic-serpent, thus a early Hellenistic manifestation of the Adversary as a bringer of knowledge, power and terror.

Scholar M. Foucart suggested that the Zeus Meilichios Serpent-god was actually Moloch (Melek) and those statues were dedicated to a foreign God, however the Adversarial manifestation of Zeus Meilichios-Maimaktes cannot be ignored.

Serpents throughout numerous ancient cultures represent wisdom and often power. Many of the Greek Gods are shown in one way or another with snakes; Asklepios, Apollo, Athene and others. Essentially, the Serpent-worship of this God was a seeming older God, yet Zeus slipped in and in a strange way absorbing the God and taking its form, thus mastering and assuming the power of it. This is a suitable example of initiation and transformation, while overcoming this chthonic form; you merely add it to you, understand, respect its nature and utilize this power within yourself. Thus it eliminates the childish need to categorize it as "good" and "evil".

We see here the relevance of the smashing of duality and the purpose of Adversarial Ritual to empower, rather than a mere curse or negative application. The "gloom and chill" ritual of Zeus Meilichios performed when the Sun may not witness it draws close similarities to the Daevayasna rites to Ahriman wherein wolf blood, omomi and other herbs are offered to the Gods of Darkness during the hours of night.

Zeus Maimaktes

AN INVOCATION TO ZEUS – DAIMON

You may begin the offering as with the initial prayer to Zeus.

I call forth unto the Daimon, Zeus.

Thee, powerful mighty ruling Daimon dread

I call to thee, Archon Zeus, life-giving, Adversary, who commands and brings Order and the source of all:

Zeus, much wandering, terrible and strong, to whom revenge and tortures dire belong.

Mankind from thee in plenteous wealth abound, when in their dwellings joyful thou art found; or pass through life afflicted and distressed, the needful means of bliss by thee suppressed.

Rise through me, Zeus Daimon alone, endued with boundless might, to keep the keys of sorrow and delight.

O holy blessed father of the Fire of Heaven, hear my prayer, disperse the seeds of life-consuming care, with favoring mind the sacred rites attend, and grant to life a glorious blessed end and gather my mind to that which shall guide me strong! Hail Father of the Empyrean, Zeus!

HADES

Hades, also known as Haides and Aidoneus is the King of the Underworld, the lord of the dead and the dark places of wisdom. Hades presides over the rites of the dead and welcomes shades into the palace of darkness. Hades is also the patron God of the wealth hidden in the earth, gold and more. In a Luciferian perspective, Hades also represents hidden knowledge and power. Persephone is the bride of Hades, half of the year she is enthroned next to him in the dark underworld.

Hades is normally depicted as a strong, dark-bearded God. As Aidoneus enthroned in the gloomy underworld, he holds a raven-tipped scepter. As Plouton or Pluto, he is a bringer of wealth and fertility. Hades is the God of Hidden Wisdom and the Riches on the depths. Hades also possess a helmet which makes the wearer invisible. His disposition is said to be fierce, violent and quick to anger.

Hades held as a symbol of power, like Hermes a staff which could command the shades to the underworld. Upon riding up from the underworld, Hades has taken a golden chariot driven by four black immortal horses. The furies are his daughters, being vampiric-death causing daimons.

The Greeks had knowledge of Black-Alchemy, of the primal magick which the deep caverns and bowels of the earth allowed the growth of crops and life, thus is the very same with individuals and magickal ascension.

The son of Cronus and Rhea, Hades is the brother of Zeus and Poseidon. Hades was given kingship over the darkness of night, wherein is the abode of shades, which he is absolute. In this aspect, Hades is called ZEUS KATACHTHONIOS or "Infernal Zeus". Another title he bares is ANAE ENERON or "King of the Shades". Hades is able to ascend to Mount Olympus as well when he so desires, yet when he is in his own kingdom he is virtually unaware of the conduct of the earth. Those who seek communion with Hades traditionally pound the earth, offer votives to him in dark places and through communion with the ERINNYES.

Those who sacrificed to Hades traditionally offered black male and femal sheep; those who offer unto Hades or Persephone were traditionally to turn their head away. Luciferians who offer to Hades respect and acknowledge his power is great, yet they must be willing to face it and assume it within themselves. Thus, Luciferians offering incense and meat offerings should face respectfully the offering to Hades.

Herakles is the only one who sought a war with Hades or Death, in Pylos which is said by some as the Gates of Hell itself. The name of Hades is said to invoke fear and hold significant power merely by vibrating it. It is significant to understand that Hades is not the Judeo-Christian Satan, his role is much deeper and without specific destructive connotation. The development of Greek mythology and religion is much more inclined to the human psyche than the stiff-necked religion of Judeo-Christianity.

When seeking the inspiration of Hades or seeking the shades of the dead, burn incense, use a black or white candle and start the working in the hours of night.

Pound the bare earth beneath you and with each strike speak "Hades".

Hades the God of the Underworld

INVOCATION OF HADES

To Pluto, Plouton, Who realms are profound and
beneath the solid ground

Hail to thou Shadow-King, ridden with deathlike cold

In the Tartarean abode away from the sight of man

Wrapped forever in the Depths of Night

To ZEUS KHTHONIOS, accept my divine rites, hear my
voice

Accept these sacred rites, through my spirit, mind and
body

Awaken and rise up in me, open forth thy gates and
lend me the

Keys to the Earth

O thou Illustrious King

Unto dread Akheron, depths obscure where roots are
nourished

Glory bright, God of the Wise open forth thy burning
eyes

Awaken and stir through me Hades!

By the Helm of Hades which brings the invisible spirit!

In your hand the Royal Scepter of Death and Darkness
come!

By Aiakos whose keys open the doors of the
Underworld!

OF NECROMANCY AND THE POWER OF HADES

Hades and Persephone are known to preside over the oracles of the dead known as NEKROMANTEIA. The oracle is one who is like a modern "medium" or one who the spirits of the deceased communicate with. Spirits may be sought by one using traditional divination techniques; however this is not a very stable process for many. Seeking spiritual communication is a practice which may provide useless for high initiatory aims, unless the obtainment of knowledge and power are a focus point. The following ritual may be conducted to gain a communion with the shades of the dead, the structure and form of the rite is from ancient Greek hymns, so it is more accurate than medieval rites. It has been adapted to a simplistic and easy to perform working. Goals for such a working should be the establishment and knowledge of an afterlife, a spiritual survival.

PERFORMANCE OF NECROMANCY POINTS

You will need a small black mirror, sulfur, jasmine and frankincense to burn near altar, a statue of Hades and Persephone. A small amount of Milk and Honey mixed in a jar, then a small container of water separate from the rest. You will need a pack of warm, bloody meat as well to offer down to the Gods of Darkness, unless of course you plan to kill a black ewe. It is best to just purchase a small pack of red meat at your local grocery shop.

In a suitable meditative position, close your eyes and allow your imagination to fuel your workings. Many of the dead are indeed flitting shadows, much of their substance of being lost.

See now with your minds' eye being upon a black sea, going forth and sailing through a rive called Okeanos, a marrow strand shall be before you and groves of Persephone. Come forth and walk through the black poplars and the willows, you will see shadows all around you.

Through the dark domain you shall come forth to the gates of Hades, yet no Cerberus to greet you. He is strangely absent. Once these things are seen allow your eyes to open. In you place of meditation you may stand up and recite the invocation. Then calmly, take the two containers – milk, honey and water – go outside and pour the libation into the ground where you make your offerings. The meat will be placed in the ground accordingly, with the blood allowed to enter and sink deep in the soil. You may feel strangely at this, yet allow yourself to feel the impressions of the spirits. Upon closing the working, thank Hades for the wisdom and retire to sleep. You may have haunting or poltergeist activity afterwards for a day or so. Keep record of it. Using recording devises for EVP will prove useful as well.

You may additionally make offerings to Persephone along with Hades for those female spirits or shades you may seek, Persephone holds this power as well.

RITES OF NEKROMANKIA

SACRED TO REX UMBRARUM

I hit now the earth and call unto the Sunless Palace of Hades

Hear my voice lord of the dead!

In the Tartarean abode away from the sight of man

Wrapped forever in the Depths of Night

To ZEUS KHTHONIOS, accept my offering

That you and your Goddess Persephone may open the gates

Of the Shades and let one imbued with spiritual life come forth

To communicate with me

I offer Milk, Honey and Water to thee!

I offer meat to thee, I look to you with this sacrifice!

Come thou souls of the Dead!

O nation of the dead, I open the gates to rise up!

I offer you blood and meat, honey and milk to thee!

I give you water to drink that you may again gain energy!

Without circle, without restrain, come thou forth shades unto me!

Hades, Lord of Avernus, who has sunk below the river Ismenos

Where it mingles with the depths

Who is strewn around with the torn entrails of sheep

Hail HEKATE, who holds power over the realm of the dead!

Hail the sacred fires of Hekate!

Three fires for the maidens born of Acheron

A fire for thee Hades, Lord of Avernus

Let the blood be offered to thee, drink deep O shades of the dead

Like the fires which burn with devouring fire

ABODES OF TARTARUS, I SEEK THEE!

Open the Darkened Palaces of the Underworld!

Throw open in answer to my knowing

The silent places and empty void of stern Persephone,

And send forth the multitude that lurk in hollow night!

Upon your offering, recite:

I offer to the Triple form of Night, O Pale Hekate!

I have given offering and prayer to Hekate, Goddess of Stygian abode!

To thee Dark Ferryman Kharon, eldritch daimon of death

From the Opening of the Mouth of Orcus come forth!

I call forth to the Oracle Daimons of Amphiaraus and Trophonios,

Grant me the knowledge of which I speak!

Hades enthroned

PERSEPHONE

Despoina, the Goddess Persephone shares the Throne of Hades, for she too is a power of the gloomy realm of the dead. It is Persephone who also has the dread power over the head of Medusa the Gorgon, for she can cast it unto those she seeks. Persephone, the Queen of the Underworld is the Daughter of Demeter. Kore, the Goddess of Spring's bounty, Persephone was kidnapped by Hades to be his bride in the underworld. Demeter searched for Persephone in the Underworld with the Torches and help of Hekate.

Persephone is the infernal goddess of death; she is known to be a daughter of Zeus and Styx as well. She is the formidable queen of the Shades, for she is able to empower the curses of men upon the spirits of the dead. She is also able to empower the curses of darkness through men in a Luciferian outlook or interpretation. Asphodel is the sacred plant of the Underworld and Persephone.

Of the many names of the Goddess can we see also Auerna, Stygia, Despoena yet also Juno Inferna. While worshipped in Arcadia under the name Despoena, she is the daughter of Poseidon and Demeter who was raised with knowledge and power by the Titan Anytus, a Daimon who appeared as a young warrior adorned in hoplite armor.

PERSEPHONE

Unto whom is Offered Libations to bring Dark Wisdom

Persephone, I call

Persephone I beckon to you

Look upon me and my offerings to you and bring forth my desire

From the Palace of the Dead send forth her shade!

That I may commune with her (my relative or dead love)

That she may bring me a sign and symbol

By dream or waking life

I call you by your names:

Khthonia, Goddess of Earth!

Megala Thea Persephone!

Daeira whose knowledge is great!

KORE Look unto me!

Juno Inferna!

Averna, Bride of Hades!

So it shall be!

Apollyon the Angel of the Bottomless Pit

APOLLO FAR-STRIKER
APOLLYON THE DESTROYER

Apollon as with most Gods has a dark side, a shadowside which further enriches his character and depth of being. Apollo as the plague spreader and death sending is "Far-Striker", for his arrows send death where he wills. Apollo kills his enemies with no regret nor fear.

Apollon is suggested to be the Judeo-Christian Abaddon or Apollyon. Hebrew: *Abaddon*, Greek: *Apollyon*, Latin: *Exterminans*, Coptic: *Abbaton*, which means "A place of destruction", "The Destroyer", "Depths of Hell" in the Revelation of St. John, Apollyon is the King of locust swarm and the angel of the bottomless pit. Louis Ginzburg in "The Legends of the Jews" defines that Abaddon is a level of hell "Hell has seven divisions, one beneath the other. They are called Sheol, Abaddon, Beer Shahat, Tit ha-Yawen, Sha'are Mawet, Sha'are Zalmawet, and Gehenna. Abaddon is presented in "The Bible of the Adversary" as a specific Qlippothic level of sorcerous power and understanding.

The anchor bible dictionary draws connection between Apollo and Apollyon, referencing that the Angel of the Bottomless Pit as Apollyon the text reads "Apollo," being the Greek god of death and pestilence as well as of the sun, music, poetry, herds, and medicine. The ancient Greek writings verb apollymi or apollyo, means "destroy." The locust was said to an emblem of this god, who poisoned his victims, and the name **"Apollyon"** may be used allusively in Revelation to attack the pagan god and so indirectly the Roman emperor Domitian, who liked to be regarded as Apollo incarnate, just as Nero considered himself as the embodiment of Apollo-Helios "The God of Light".

Emperor Domitian

The New Moon or Dark Moon was a festival night for Apollo. The Lord of the Silver Bow could send darts of death when he wished; none could subdue them nor avert them. Often, "Paian" was the name given to a battle-chant before going forth to kill, it was offered to Apollo to avert death and pestilence upon them, for his power could avert and send. When the Gallic hordes descended upon the Delphian temple a great storm broke forth, stones rolling down thwarting the Gauls which sent them away in fear of the God.

Apollo appears in the colder months sometimes as a ravening wolf in front of his temple at Delphi. Zeus was also called a wolf-god as well; however Apollo appeared in this form as the destroying god. Apollo would brandish a golden sword as the destroying force as well.

Judeo-Christianity has done a good job with 'fleshing out' the daemonic aspects of Apollo, as some illustrations here will display. Please consider that as Apollo is destructive he is also life-affirming and indulges in the beauty of light.

Apollyon the King of the Bottomless Pit with Plague Arrow, draconian wings and serpent-like body

Apollyon bearing plague arrow in Dragon form from old Christian text. The Luciferian or Dark Pagan should be cautious in utilizing daemonic or primal imagery, to avoid being caught in derogatory Judeo-Christian negativity. Look to the symbolism as the destroyer as an aspect of the creator.

THE CALLING OF THE ANGEL OF THE BOTTOMLESS PIT, APOLLYON

For the rites of cursing and dark knowledge

Discord and unturned chaos turned,

Thou beautiful one adorned in the serpent consumed skin,

Who by slaying commanding the essence therein

I call thee forth, Angel of the Bottomless Pit,

Never deformed yet terrible in appearance

Armed with arrows dread: far-striking,

Bakkhion, twofold and divine, power far diffused,

and course oblique is thine.

In one hand stands forth the Golden Sword of Vengence

In the other the Silver-Bow of plague and death

Open the pit and send forth pestilence, let thy locusts consume

I curse thee………. in the name of Apollyon……..place thy mask of darkness

Upon thy beautiful face……become the crooked angel of pestilence

….name…. I curse your Eyes, may they fog with shadows of your failure and regret, …name… I curse your mind that it may be tormented by the locusts-daimons of the underworld, …name…I curse your limbs that they may ache with old age yet so early, ...name... I send forth Apollyon's arrow to your heart to make it a home for worms and decay, ...name... I offer you and sacrifice you in the name of Apollyon, that you may go forth to the bottomless pit in darkness.

Burn or stab image repeatedly. Make offering to Apollyon Far-Striker.

Dark knowledge oracle:

I call unto thee, Apollyon O thou Angel of both Darkness and Light,

Rise up through me Apollon Lykios

Who sends the wolf upon the herds

Rise up and accept my offering!

I seek the forbidden knowledge, that of the serpent!

O Apollon Lykios, in thy form chosen grant me thy insight!

Apollyon the Angel of the Bottomless Pit

Apollo Far-Striker sending plague arrow

Antiochus IV Epiphanes as Apollo from coin

MEFITIS / MEPHITIS

Mefitis was the Roman daemoness of the personification of poisonous gases emitted from the ground, particularly in swamps and volcanic vapors. Her name is suggested to mean "noxious" and relates to her as a fearful chthonic daimon. Mefitis or Mephitis is empowered by the sulphurous fumes and was at times considered a plague goddess.

Mefitis in her Goddess aspect associates her with Albunea who was a prophetic nymph or Sibyl-like Daimon who lived in the sulfuric spring close to Tivoli, she even had a temple. Albunea was called the "tenth Sibyl" by Lactantius and mentioned Albunea was worshipped at Tibur. Her image holding a book was found in the river bed of Anio. Her sortes were at the command of the Roman senate and were kept in the Capitol. The name Albunea is derived from albinus, "white" and refers to the sulfurous water at her spring. She was considered one of the Pegaeae.

The ruined temple of Apollo at Avernus held precedence as this area was considered a gateway to Hades, or the Underworld. The Mefitis vapors were considered so dangerous that birds could not fly above them. The Mefitis Goddess was highly feared and yet she held the qualities of being able to keep certain sickness away as well.

Mefitis was worshipped at Potentia, Grumentum, Transapadane Gaul however her cult was strongest in central Italy. An inscription during the time of Septimius

Severus makes references to her temple being a bit north of the Temple of Juno Lucina, the bride of Jupiter.

In the civil war of 69 AD, Tacitus wrote concerning the slaughter of Cremona and that although nearly every sacred and profane building was burnt and destroyed, a single temple was left standing. It was the Temple of Mefitis.

One may seek Mefitis for improving health and lung problems, meditating and calling upon her with burning sulfur and heavy vapors. She may be offered to by way of burning sulfur.

Stephen Flowers wrote in his "The Secrets of Fire and Ice, A Historical Supplement to the text" that in the essay "Mephistopheles oder Luzifer?" by Gregor Gregorius that Mephistopheles is interpreted as the Greek word meaning "He who does not love the light" yet also the Hebrew Mephir "destroyer" and tophel "Liar". The female daemon Mefitis was sacrificed to like other subterranean Gods and Goddesses according to Gregorius, as well as orgies and human sacrifice. It is Gregorius who suggested that Mephistopheles is from "Mefitis-o-philos" being "Mephistopheles".

HEKATE

Hecate or Hekate is the Goddess of Witchcraft, night, sorcery, the moon and necromancy. Considered the child of Perses and Asteria she was crowned with the power over heaven, earth and sea. Traditionally, Hecate is shown as a woman holding two torches and wearing a knee-length maiden skirt and hunting boots, similar to Artemis. Hecate developed further in her role as being the pale goddess of night, whose power resided not only in Heaven yet also the underworld and the crossroads. Her triple form as Maiden-Mother-Crone announces her power as a Goddess over the Feminine mysteries.

Further explanation indicates that Hecate was originally a Titan, ancient and before many as well as an ancient Thracian divinity. She was said to have ruled in heaven, the earth and from the sea who she was able to bestow wealth to mortals. She was the only Titan who was able to retain this power with Zeus.

Hecate is a mystic goddess, for her powers are so extensive that they were even celebrated in Samothrace and Aegina. She was often identified with Demeter, Cybele and Rhea. A close line of association was also found with Artemis and Persephone as well due to their role as Goddesses of both Hunting and the Moon. Hecate's traditional symbol in modern times in the Triple Moon which represents the powers of the moon, underworld and feminine mysteries.

Hekate is also called the mother of Skylla, a sea-monster therefore being the same as Krataeis. She is

found as being the same as Skylakagetis which means (leader of dogs). Hekate is considered the consort of the Khthonian Hermes in the cults of Thessalian Pherai and Eleusis. Both are leaders of the shades of the dead and assisted in the spring-time return of Persephone each year.

Hecate's power overtime extended to the Underworld, where she rules as a mighty divinity which hold sway over the souls of the departed. She is accompanied by Stygian gods and wolves.

Regarded as a Spectral Daimon, she during the hours of night sent forth from the lower world demons and terrible phantoms who taught and initiated others into the mysteries of sorcery and witchcraft, holding power and dwelling in the places where two roads crossed. Dwelling also in tombs they grew stronger where the split blood of murdered persons is.

Hekate wanders about with the souls of the dead; the howling of dogs signifies her approach. The appearance of Hecate is terrible; she appears as a woman with three bodies or three heads. One may be that of a horse, the second a dog and the third a lion.

In traditional left hand path, chaos magic or Luciferian circles she is a glyph of the primal power of magick and the sorcerous path of Sabbatic mysteries. Hecate holds power of the Tri-fold power of the infernal and empyrean.

Traditional offerings to Hecate may be dogs, black lambs and honey at the crossroads. Luciferians or modern practitioners often use the blood of the moon (female cycle), blood of the sorcerer offering, honey, rose and rose water, human bone dust that is poured or offered at a site designated to her under the Dark Moon (sorcerous workings) or the Full Moon (magickal or Olympian prayers).

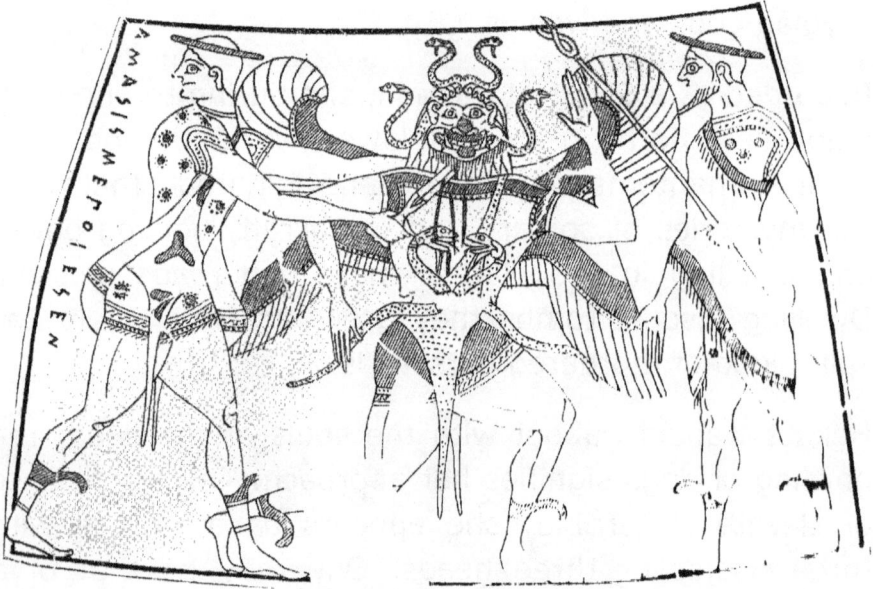

Medusa the Gorgon

INVOCATION TO HEKATE

By Torch-bearing Hekate, Thou Holy Daughter of great-
bosomed Nyx

I summon thee by blood, by honey and by rose

O Goddess of Howling Dogs and Gorgon's cries in the
hours of night

Hekate Einodia, Trioditis,

lovely dame, of earthly, watery, and celestial frame,

sepulchral, in a saffron veil arrayed,

pleased with dark ghosts that wander through the
shade;

Perseis, solitary goddess, hail!

The world's key-bearer,

Never doomed to fail;

In stags rejoicing, huntress,

Nightly visioned, and drawn by bulls,

Unconquerable queen;

Leader, Nymphe, nurse, on mountains wandering

Whose torches bear the Black Flame of Illumination

I have the courage to witness thy Holy Rites

Howling Goddess

She who appears holding the Serpent,

Whose Cruelly Sharp blade seeks the throats of your offerings

Who is the Maiden – Mother – Crone of the Path of the Moon

Who bears the terrible and ghostlike shapes

Whose faces reflect the moon upon water

Whose pale visage reveals

Whose faces are Black Dog, Horse and the Lion

Hecate, look upon my offerings with pleasure

For I am a child of your primal and glorious power

By three Nights I call thee as Selene's Bright Horns meet

Exalted above shadow, she who inspires darkness

Shown in fullest radiance and of hag-phantomed night

When the moon is hungering for the blood of the maiden

Hail thou Hekate, illuminate me with your Torches of Wisdom

Serpent-coiled Black Moon, Horned Moon and Full Radiance!

HECATE WHO CARRIES THE TORCH

A Conjuration and Offering to the Goddess in Three Phases

In your somber beauty, Youthful passion and Goddess-inspired wisdom

I call unto you thou Hecate of the Three Ways

Who is all seeing of night

O Artemis Regina Nemorum

Who in solitude lovest thy mountain-haunts, whose talons

Tear through and fangs revealing hungering immortal soul

Holy Goddess, empower my life with your strength and nocturnal wisdom

O Bright Orb of Heaven, Selene of the Beautiful Night

Whose Moon-beams shall bring forth all phantoms of night

By the Toad-path and guidance of the forbidden

O three-formed Hecate, whose torches at hand

Bring unto me and within the Black Flame of your Wisdom

Who powers are endless, who controls thirsting clouds of spirits

---

Whose pale ghost-like face illuminates down with shadow

From undimmed Horns

Artemis – Hekate – Selene of thy Holy Names

Triple Goddess, of many turnings who guides the silver chariot

Which drakons slither according to thy desires

Lend to me thy Mystic Torch

Nightwanderer, staghunter Artemis

Witch-Mother Hekate

Bright-Moon and Holy Horned Goddess Selene!

I summon thee to look favorable upon my desire!

So it is done!

KAKODAIMONES

Cacodaemon is an "evil spirit" ancient Demonological literature. A Kakodaimon is considered in many esoteric cases to be associated with man, each one being a part of the psyche. The human also possesses what is called a Agathoi Daimon which is a gift giving good spirit. In the left hand path cosmology, the Luciferian understands that the Kakodaimon and Agathoidaimon are one and that both may be balanced in magickal assumption. Achieving congress with the Daimon may be done by many different means, depending on the individual.

MANIA

Goddess of the Dark Sorcery Moon

Mania is the Etruscan Goddess of the Underworld, who is essentially considered the Mother of Manes or Manei and Larei/Lares. Mania's power was feared, for she cast madness upon humans.

The Temple of Mania was located in the land between Arcadia and Messenia and it was the Romans who adopted her from the Etruscans. Mania's magick was centered on gloom and darkness; she was very close in form to Medusa-Gorgon, for like the Romans, Medusa's head was adorned on items for good luck much like the Etruscans.

The cult of sacrifice and offerings made to Mania around the time of the Romans was boiled beans, yet also her cult was related to human heads, severed as offerings. The heads were significant as Etruscans believed the human spirit dwelled in the head. In later practice, onions or garlic was used instead of heads as offerings to the Mistress of the Protoocean, where all things dissolved. Luciferians or left hand practitioners do not recognize the significance of the Protoocean as the goal is the continuation of consciousness and achieving the possibility of spiritual immortality.

Mania was offered to on the same date as Luperk, the Wolf God or Favn/Pan in which she held power over the chthonic realms and the Wolf God and Pan relating to herds and fertility. As Mania was offered to on the same date as the God Vulcan is found in the chthonic aspect of the shadow, the fire within which causes change. May 1st is a suitable time to offer to Mania, while you may do so in addition with offerings to Hecate as well.

CHARON

The demon of death of Etruscan mythology, Charu, is the same as the Greek Charon, who led souls of the deceased across the river Styx. Charu is shown on tombs as a witness to the death of humanity; his power however seems to be varied. Appearing as a fiery haired demon, he has a hooked nose similar to a beak of a bird of prey, feathered wings and often a long handled hammer. Often, Charon is shown with burning eyes, Charu was not shown as a guide to the dead in Etruscan lore. His hammer, the symbol of death presents him as a murderous demon often in the company of Cerebrus, the beast of death who guarded Hades. Some images of Charu presents him as wearing a lion headdress, symbolic of fierce death. His blue-gray skin, often serpent-draped arms present him as a powerful force of physical death and initiatory survival.

Traditional lore presents Charon as the boatman who takes souls to Hades, traditionally a coin in placed in the mouth which the soul offers to Charon. Those unable to pay Charon roam about as ghosts.

TUHULKA

The Etruscan Tuhulka / Tuchlucha is a grotesque demon with a vultures beak holding snakes in his hands. His head often manifests as a vulture, he is the destruction or consumption of the soul. He often appears with Charu and both have a strong connection to each other, both daemons execute the Will of the Gods of Darkness or the Underworld. Left Hand Path practitioners as a power of determined Will, or the manifestation of accomplishment. In offering to the shades of the underworld and Gods of Darkness, a coin for each daemons – Tuhulka and Charu should be placed in a graveyard in seeking communion with the spirits.

Tuchulcha lived in the underworld and has hair made of serpents with the ears of a horse or donkey. Tuchulcha holds a staff and pitchfork and is often violent.

Cronus – Saturn the Cannibal God

CRONUS – KRONUS

Cronus is the Titan God of time and endless existence, attributed to Saturn and often the Mithraic concept of death and immortality. Kronos gained rule of the cosmos by deposing his father Ouranos (the sky). Upon gaining rule for an extended period of time, a prophecy came to Cronus that his son would overthrow him; he through the instinct of survival devoured his children one by one. Rhea-Cybele saved Zeus by hiding. It was later that Zeus fought against the titans, causing Cronus to disgorge them and then sealed Cronus in the pit of Tartaros.

Saturnus / Cronus is often shown as a bearded man who holds a scythe or sickle. The Luciferian and left hand path interpretation is that Cronus is within each man, Zeus included, that all are born with the instinct of survival and cruel applications therein. It is our duty to keep them within boundaries until there is a need for less restriction.

Survival instinct is a Luciferian trait which causes the individual to grow stronger and perhaps more powerful over time. Let's consider Phraates IV, the Great Parthian ruler who battled and defeated Marc Anthony. Having come from a large family, Phraates IV usurped the throne by killing his father and then murdering his 30+ brothers and their families to secure his position as King. Backed by the Scythians, Phraates IV was considered a cruel king who later made peace with Augustus Caesar and even returned some Roman eagles taken during battles. His instinct for power and survival are admirable traits, we can only assume the situation he was placed in from which he had to make tough decisions like exterminating his father and brothers. In ancient times, if one was killed the family would remain a long enemy, always being a sublime threat to the victor.

Phraates IV crowned by Nike from coin

Antiochus IV Epiphanies gained his throne by killing the infant relative of his, then having the assassin in turn killed for treason to avoid loose ends. Antiochus IV Epiphanies maintained the Seleucid Empire despite having many difficulties within and outside of his Empire. During his lifetime, he maintained it. Antiochus even nearly conquered Egypt and if Rome had not stepped in, he would have been King of Egypt as well! If this is not Seth manifest, the God of Foreign lands, then what is?

Kronus is a primal, harsh and cannibalistic God. He will not be willingly overthrown, if by any means he will overcome even if he must against something he loves.

A Veiled Kronus from Roman Emperor Domitian Coin

Cannibalism and Vampirism are always considered aspects of primal instinct and the desire to ascend into Godhood, continual self-development and mastering all things in your life. While cannibalism and vampirism are not widely practiced in civilized society, the symbolism of such demonstrates the origins of our being.

TELCHINES

The Telchines are said to be a tribe descended from Poseidon based on the concept that they are four magickian-smiths and sea-daimons that dwelt near Rhodes and made weapons. They created the sickle used by Kronos and gave Poseidon the trident he was able to use to level mountains and destroy large amounts of people. This is one of the balanced aspects of Poseidon, he could create and destroy based on his will alone. Zeus at one point had the Telchines taken to the depths of Tartaros.

The Telchines had a great power as sorcerous daimons, being able to create storms and such chaos as they so desired. They cast their storms upon Khaos the Wind, from which it grew stronger and traveled. Their eyes alone could be destructive, they were able to assume any other form they wished as well. One aspect of their sorcery was to mix Stygian water and sulfur, then able to use it to destroy animals and plants according to their desire.

These Sons of Poseidon were six Daimons of the Sea who haunted the dark caverns of the island of Rhodes. Apollo once took the form of a destructive wolf to destroy or calm the actions of the Telchines as well. One of these Sea-Daimons were said to have built the Temple of Apollo at Lycia.

Their weapons made inspired others to Bakkhic frenzy and took the form of hooded ministers, inspiring terror during their celebrative rites by war-dances, chaos-flute music and howling.

EURYNOMUS

Eurynomus is a netherworld Daimon (meaning spirit) of decaying corpses and dead matter. He strips flesh from the bones of the dead and feeds on human carrion specifically. He is king over flies, maggots and vultures. Eurynomus is commonly depicted with blue-black skin and wearing a cloak made of vulture-hide. It is said that the Delphian guides mentioned Eurynomus as being one of the Daimones associated with Hades. This Daimon of death survived as a medieval demon described as Eurynome, yet held the same aspects of the ancient Greek Eurynomus.

HECATONCHEIRES

The Hecatoncheires where violent storm gods who could be summoned from the pits of Tartaros, they had each a hundred hands and fifty heads which they used to yield and send forth violent storms. They were brothers to Kyklopes who crafted the thunder and lightning of Zeus.

SKYLLA

Scylla or Skylla is a daimon-sea Goddess who inspires terror and haunts the rocks near a whirpool daemon called Kharybdis. She has ravenous, darting heads and is a monstrous form with twelve feet, six heads lined with a triple row of teeth. Her voice is said to sound like a yelping dog and is has parts which resemble a hermit crab or some type of sea creature.

LAMIA

Lamia, the Queen of Libya who was loved by the God Zeus and was cursed by Hera. She was the daughter of the God Poseidon and was the mother of Skylla. Upon her curse by Hera, Zeus initiated Lamia into darkness and gave her the form of a monstrous vampire-daimon who extracted her bloodlust on stealing babies and devouring their flesh and drinking their blood.

One of the known forms of Lamia is a shark-daimon, she is also mother to other demonic shark spirits who devour children.

The Empusae are terror-inspiring underworld vampires who seduced young men to drain their blood and consume their flesh. They are immortal daimons who were separated in three clases, the Empusae, the Mormolykeiai and the Lamiae, the Lamia had serpent-tails instead of legs, the Empusae had fiery hair or flaming hair and the legs of a beast like a donkey, goat or of brass.

Considered haunting shades of phasma, Lamia would assume a pleasing shape to seduce and consume the life of young men. Their queen was Hekate, for she is the Goddess of Witchcraft and ghosts and with her command came forth from the underworld.

Some of them were living women; some were ghosts of murdered of vengeful ladies. Lamia of Libya was a Queen who was loved by Zeus and cursed by Hera. Lamia became a demoness and then began taking children, draining their blood and eating their flesh. Her desire for immortality went beyond her vengeance it so seems.

The term Mormolycia as they are called means "frightful wolves" as they are terrifying and fierce in their desire to attack and consume life. Lamia, being the child-snatcher according to Bell in "Women of Classical Mythology" describes them as seducing young men to enjoy their fresh youthful energy, drinking their blood and eating their flesh to continue immortal existence in time.

The Empusae appear as ghosts and shades, gaining temporary form to draw energy from others. They go away shrieking often, howling into the darkness of night.

When performing the "Summoning of the Cloak of Strix" it is significant for the witch / sorcerer to offer to the Gods of Night, to then enter the dream focused on a goal of Sabbatic gathering.

The Hekate Dark moon with inverted pentagram represents the mastery of the spirit, flesh and mind of the practitioner and the independence as a spiritual being. This is the sigil of the Maiden – Mother – Crone Goddess who is self-reliant and accountable for her own destiny.

SUMMONING OF THE CLOAK OF STRIX

Of Nocturnal Flight and Forbidden Desires

I conjure thee, Primal Hungering Ones

Screech Owl Goddesses

Whose moon is darkened

Eclipse and ascend from Tartaros the shades of the dead

Immortal, hungering and seeking the youth for continued strength

Mormolyttomai, whose body is covered in blemishes and blotches

Whose flesh is gray and green, spider veined and black burning eyes

Whose legs are as the beast or serpent

Whose wings are like bats fluttering in the dark

Whose hair is like fire and who is strong like brass

LAMIA LIBYS, Queen of Vampires of Night

Seeking the blood and flesh of the Young

Bride of Set-Typhon, who killed and devoured the strength of Osiris

I conjure thee shade from the pits of Tartarus!

Ghostlike women of dark shadows, take the form you wish

MORMOLYKEIAI, EMPUSAE and LAMIA COME FORTH!

Let me take flight with thee to drain life and gain strength

So my secret desires be sated!

THANATOS

The winged Daimon of Death, Thanatos is called the "Black Mors". Thanatos was born of Nyx or Night. The abode of Thanatos is in Tartarus and he may take many forms, sometimes pleasing and other times horrifying. Thanatos may be called forth or offerings made for spirit-journeys or meditating on the nature of the self or subconscious mind.

INVOCATION OF THANATOS

I call unto the Shadow of Peaceful Death

Whom often follows his brother Hypnos

Thou Thanatos, whose death's shadow brings forth and encircles

With a dark cloud

Come forth to me and empower me with the sight of shadow

I offer to thee Honey and Libations, without a shade to give

Let me descend by dream after the touch of your bother Hypnos

The Shadowy place of the dead

That I shall pass the Black Gates which hold back thou shades

Of Hades and Persephone I call

Send to me the messenger of Oneiroi..

The traditional Hekate Sigil, the Triple Moon representing the Goddess in all of her aspects, both light and dark.

HERMES KHTHONIUS

Hermes Chthonius is the 'shadowside' or dark aspect of Hermes as the Guide of the Dead who leads souls to Hades. Hermes is significant in this role as his power concerning Magick is often perceived greater than the traditional Hermes. The Luciferian tradition itself was fueled by Satanist Charles Pace who wrote that Anubis in the Egyptian Funerary tradition is Hermanubis, the Opener of the Way or initiator of the shadow path.

Hermes Chthonius is connected to the Greek funerary cult in a magickal practice involving a vase or spirit container called a PITHOIGIA or PITHOI. One specific funerary vase at Aphidna in the Dipylon Cemetery shows Hermes Chthonius or Hermes Psychopomps using his magick wand to revoke souls or Keres from ascending upward, thus his power as a sorcerer established in the shadow cult. This vase is labeled "Out of the doors, ye souls; it is no longer Anthesteria". The Pithoigia of the Anthesteria is a form of the primitive Pithoigia of the grave-jars.

Hermes Psychopomps (pompos means conductor) is known as the Evoker and Revoker of souls and shades of the dead. Hermes is shown holding two specific wands, yet only using one. He holds the Caduceus or Herald's Staff, representing wisdom and divine (or infernal) power, the other he holds a rhabdos which is a magick wand. The difference between the Rhabdos and Kerykeion is that the Kerykeion or Caduceus is the King's Scepter held by the herald as deputy, thus power invested. The Rhabdos is a simple wand and is an enchanter's wand.

Hermes Chthonius used the rhabdos to lead the shades of the dead to Hades. It is in this instance that the wand became an attribute and useful item in rites of necromancy and holding sway over the dead. The rites of Zeus Maimakterion used the rhabdos performed ceremonies of sending forth. Over the ages both the rhabdos and Caduceus became fused and utilized as one.

Hermes Chthonius may be invoked by those wishing to perform workings of communication with the shades of the dead or necromancy, offerings of frankincense and myrrh.

The consideration that Thoth was Hermes was deemed inaccurate by Charles M. Pace. In the Book of Tahuti (Thoth), a grimoire of the Tarot, Pace describes that Hermes and Death is Anubis (messenger). Anpu is the Opener of the Way, the Lord of Jackals. The Greeks called him Hermanubis.

Hermes Khthonius with Caduceus and wand with Daimon-Keres, Daimons of the Underworld.

INVOCATION OF HERMES KHTHONIUS

I invoke thee Hermes Khthonius

Hermes I invoke, I call thee forth

Whom fate decrees to dwell near to Kokytos

The stream of Hades

Bakkheios Hermes

Progeny of the Divine Dionysos, father of the vine

Of Celestial Aphrodite, Paphian queen

Dark eye lashed Goddess

Who wanders the sacred seats where Hades dread empress retreats

Hail thou Hermes Khthonius, shadow dweller and power of guidance

Who knows and adores Tartaros dark and wide

Giving it forever flowing souls to guide

Come, Blessed power

Thy sacrifice attend

Come now, Hermes Khthonios!

Hermes

KERES & GORGON

The Daimons of Violent Death, their strike is cruel. They preside over the more violent forms of death, war, murder are what they thirst for. These female daimons who craved blood and thrived upon it. They are vampires in every way, haunting most frequently battlefields. They ripped the soul free from the body and fed upon its blood.

Such Daimons of the Underworld, Keres have a multiplied and similar power of the yatukih-persian Astovidad, the Death-Daimon from which none may escape.

The Keres are associated with the Daimon of Nightmare, Hepiales. The Keres are powerful, yet some just flitter about like flies. Blindness, madness may be caused by Keres before death in some cases.

Keres are considered dangerous to plants, some emerging from the ground and some from the air. In addition they are able to infest fire. This holds specific interest to the common-associated Yatukih of ancient Persia, corrupting the fire of the Zoroastrian cult with spittle, breath, hair and nail clippings which are offerings to demons or daevas.

In Greek religious practice, Philo and a commentator write that no profane fire should touch the religious altar, else it become infested with Keres. The word Keres is suggested to mean darkening, killing, eclipse and spiritual corruption.

In addition Keres holds a significant interest in the left hand path, as it is a word related to the Telchines and other magicians of Antiquity. Strabo writes that Keres tended to become exhalted and personified into literal magicians. There is a section from Stesichorus quoted by Eustathius that mentions there was an ancient tribe of the Kouretes, who were Cretans and called Thelgines. These people or some of them were magickians and sorcerers. There are two types traditionally, some craftsmen and skilled in handiwork others were of a fierce nature and were favored to be the origins of squalls of wind, they had a cup or chalice in which they would brew potions from roots.

These Keres who were of the "darker" type created statuary and metals which were amphibious and daemonic in nature. Some were demons, others like fish, others like serpents and others with no hands or feet. Many had webs between their fingers like geese and they were blue-eyed and black-tailed. This older group of sorcerers and magickians were struck down by Zeus or Apollo according to legend, similar to the tales of Tiamat and Marduk.

In one specific figure Herakles is shown striking down a daemonic – old man type of Keres, showing the mastery of the self. Homor described the Ker of Death is half-death, half-death-spirit thus possessing isolate intelligence.

Keres, having been sorcerers and magickians in life, seem to have been granted specific roles and powers upon their initiation by Zeus and Apollo, according to mythology.

Keres are similar to Harpies, called the Snatchers, winged-women daimons who carry along souls to Hades. Keres, Harpies and Gorgons are often crossed in mythology, demonstrating a deeper significance to their form and purpose. In Hesiod the "black Ker" is the sister of Thanatos and the Moros (doom) and the tribe of dreams. (theog.211 Hes.).

The Gorgon is a form of the Keres, phantoms which dwelled in Hades; the Gorgon was most famous for Medusa, who could at times appear beautiful. The three Gorgons of myth are Stheion, Euryale and Medusa. They dwelt in Libya and are physically described as being girded with serpents all about their heads, raising their tongues and gnashing their teeth. The Gorgons have wings and brazen claws with razor sharp teeth.

Athena had the power to initiate and transform those of darkness, it is said that she gave Medusa the hair of serpents. The blood of Gorgons sprang the serpents of Libya. Daemonic powers had long be associated with serpents. Azhi Dahaka, Ahriman's great powerful storm-demon had the ability when his blood was split to also bleed forth serpents and other beasts. In a Prussian Vampire-Tale, the Vampire burnt on a pyre dissipated and his spirit escaped as various salamanders and vipers.

Being demonic beings, they were not without their charms. Posidon who would be surrounded by adoring sea monsters, seduced Medusa and copulated with her.

Invoking or Evoking the Keres is an initiatory experience which will fuel the process of understanding the natural cycle of death, the experience seeking knowledge of the possibility of the survival of the psyche. Invoke the Keres to understand death, to gain a spiritual connection with the necromantic power associated with it. You may use a triangle to focus the Keres in, simply naming it around to give honor to them. They are very similar to the Daevas and Druj of Yatukih Sorcery, their power is equally involving.

The Keres require blood upon summoning, you may wish to offer some of your own fresh blood or by placing it in an airtight jar for a period of time, allowing it to coagulate and rot. When the top is taken off some months later, it will smell the entire room with decay and rot. Mix this with the burning of sulfur in the chamber and you will have a proper underworld ambiance.

The path of Magick, Pagan practice or witchcraft designate from a left hand path perspective that the initiate is willing to embrace their own circumference of being, i.e. the circle as it is represented, as the beginning and end of all. This with the interpretation of the Adversary within is essential in Luciferian practice, for AZOTHOZ is that very mystery which is revealed through experience.

ENSORCELLING OF THE KERES

By the Gods of Darkness I ensorcel thee!

Dark Keres Thanatoio

I evoke thee to rise up from Tartarus Dark Ker!

Shrouded in darkness, devouring one!

I offer thee Blood to Manifest within this Circle!

Once you have gained strength you may leave its confines!

Ker the Destructive

Whose robes are blood red

I conjure thee Akhlys (death mist)

Pale, shriveled, shrunk with hunger

Swollen Kneed, blackened long nails tipped your hands

She whose cheeks blood dripped down to the ground

She or He that seeks the streams of blood

Death-demons, storm-ghosts come forth!

O thou snatchers ride the northern winds!

O thou demons of the south winds come to me!

Who Night bore hateful Moros and Black Fate

Thanatos enthroned and the bearing of Hypnos

Who resides among the tribe of dreams

I conjure thee!

Night bore the Avengers and Keres pitiless

Ascend through me Ker who lives within

Let me take my balanced command as the Adversary Incarnate!

I invoke thee, blue-black Keres, who grind their sharpened teeth

Glaring and grim, bloody and insatiable

Who strive around those who fall, greedy to drink their life

Gorge on the Black Blood, Keres lay your long claws

Take down souls and feed Hades in the gloom chill of Tartarus!

ENYO

Enyo is one of the Graiai who are ancient sea-daimons who were said to personify White Sea foam. Having gray hair from birth, they are terrible spirits to behold, much like hags. Enyo is "the warlike", Persis "the destroyer" and Deino "the terrible". Called "the old women", they were daughters of Phorcys and Ceto. The sisters had only one eye and tooth in common, which they borrowed from each other as needed.

Enyo was robed in saffron and Persis or Pemphredo was robed in beauty. The third is not described yet in other tales they are winged and commonly sisters of the Gorgons.

TYPHON /TYPHOEUS

Typhon is a name associated with *typhein meaning 'to smoke'* and is associated with typhoon, being a storm. I refer to him as the HIDDEN GOD as his power is illuminating within the other Gods; the masks of Typhon are many. ENKELADOS is also a name associated with Typhon as well, being a Giant who was placed within a mountain or volcano. The word Enkelados is means *"to urge on"* or *"sound the cry"* representing battle or strife.

Typhon or Trypheus is the son of Gaia and Tartarus who is the depths of the abyss, the God of the Pit. Typhon is the God of Wind yet is centered as a bringer of Chaos and Storm. The Luciferian may look to Typhon as being a powerful archetype or God of self-struggle and mastery of both darkness and light. In deeper Luciferian traditions, the Algol symbol of the eight pointed chaos star and inverted pentagram represent the same aspects of Typhon compared in other mythological and magickial elements.

Typhon's descriptions feature him as a powerful manifestation which brings fear to all. Typhon is a man from the waist upward and reached upward towards the stars. His hands reached east and west, from which he had 100 dragon/serpent heads on each. The viper/serpent aspect of Typhon was below his waist and had coils that could reach up above his bearded face and head. His body was covered in wings and his eyes flashed with burning, crimson black fire.

Typhon represents from a left hand path perspective the power of willed thought, the rebel spirit which first comes into light and may liberate all. Zeus is one aspect of Typhon, they are eternally linked and such is the reason why Zeus was able to master Typhon.

Typhon was born of the lust of two, Mother Earth or Gaia and Tartarus with the aid of the Golden Aphrodite, for this was sexual magick at its foundation and the illumination of Will and Knowledge. In the Homeric hymn to Apollo Typhon was the son of Hera in her Minoan form, such as the serpent goddess and a daemonic manifestation of Hephaestus in a cave.

Typhon sought to overthrow Zeus and become the Lord of Gods, which in the first battle he did overcome Zeus and eclipsed the Sun, from which the land of the dead was brought much closer to the fleshly reality we experience. This was Chaos inspired and brought forth. Such chaotic power placements are meaningful as they inspire further change and response, thus balanced in their attempt of the flowering of life itself.

Typhon was a manifestation of the primal and most powerful of forces. His nature of chaos was on the inner plane an ordered force, single minded and determined to overmaster all. A suitable left hand path or Luciferian trait, the same is viewed in Zeus except for the point that Zeus appears differently in the idol and interpretation than does Typhon. One may consider the two the same except for the process of overcoming duality, where their powers intermingle and they are illuminated in the forefront of the Gods.

Typhon is the chthonic manifestation of not only the volcanic forces of Hephaestus (the Roman Vulcan) and the very strength of the underworld and chaos, while Hades represents a mastered God and not the collective forces themselves. The hundred dragon or serpent heads continually hiss and with dark flickering tongues sense all around him, his multitude of daemonic voices echo his very speech, along with his rapid movement from the hundred serpent legs which slither him quickly to and fro.

Typhon is the God of Storms, or tsunamis and finds rest in Tartarus and under Mount Etna, where he was cast after Zeus mastered his power with lightning bolts during their long struggle. One may worship the manifestation of both Zeus and Typhon, for there is wisdom in both and their relationship. The Left hand path practitioner will notice the subtle points of initiation in the infernal and chthonic, how these directly strengthen the empyrean and the Olympian.

Typhon's bride is Echidna who is a serpent-woman Goddess and from their union are the children such as the half-woman/lion Sphinx, who is found in Egypt, the Serpent Lernaean Hydra, the two headed wolf Orthrus,

Cerebrus, the serpent-maned dog which guards the entrance to Hades and the Nemean Lion.

Typhon was such a fierce some deity that he caused all the Gods besides Zeus to flee to Egypt. They became the Egyptian Gods worshipped long ago.

Herodotus identified Typhon with Set / Seth as the God of Storms, the very power of the Cult of Storms and Darkness. It is indeed Typhon-Set who is the Hidden God of Power, the initiator and who transforms into Zeus, thus the initiate or left hand path practitioner may utilize this dual or Adversarial force to unite opposites within.

Meditations, invocations and other workings with Typhon are of a darker yet illuminating path. Typhon is a direct link to our subconscious mind, desires and possibilities within our own selves, it is the stirring power of the serpent which causes our ascension, our mastery of the storm-pits of chaos and the ascension and mastery of our inner light.

Preparation for the Invocation of Typhon should have the ritual chamber adorned in symbols of the Hidden God, if possible conducting during a storm. If you are fortunate to be in the path of a Category 2 hurricane this will prove equally exciting and empowering. The burning of sulfur, dried or clotted blood are meaningful scents attributed to Typhon.

INVOCATION OF TYPHON THE HIDDEN GOD

The Words of Opening Tartarus

Hekas, Hekas Nohpyth Bebeloi

All profane devoured, the Sun swallowed

The Moon eclipsed, yet a single flame burning

For I ascend in my own light

ZAZAS, ZAZAS, NASATANADA ZAZAS!

Crack open black hearted Stygian rocks

Let the crag of Akheron covered in gore no longer hold thee

Let my words ring forth, stirring storm

Hurricane and tsunami, darkness and chaos rise!

Typhoeus, I adore thee as the God of All

Hidden in the depths of my soul, rise up O primal darkness

Typhon, whose hands and arms are mighty

Which strike from east and west

Whose feet are that of coiled serpents and dragons, tireless!

From your shoulders there grew a hundred serpent heads

Those of a dreaded Drakon of Kaos

The heads licked with dark tongues, from the eyes shines a blackened fire

Whose heads fire from eyes piercing with a bright lantern

Exalted Lord and King of the Darkened Pits of Tartarus

Whose cloak and faces may be changed in accordance of your design

I am of your blood and touched by the fire of your spirit

Flashed with blood and the hunger of the devouring Lion, ascend!

Whose voices are the multitudes of serpents and beasts whose tongues

Vibrate the primal essence and tongue of shadows

Those words which beget future and darkened design

Whose face is fierce in countenance and illuminated by thy fiery eyes

Which reveal the Abyss and the chaos within!

Let me shape this power to my design!

Whose crown is iron and burnt black as the pits of Tartarus

Typhon-Imperator, whose halo is the lightning and storm-clouds!

Whose mouth is human, bearded yet whose teeth are of the Drakon

Whose tongue is black and flickering as the Fires within thy spirit

Whose words command the flesh and world around us

Typhon who issues a great storm of fire from his mouth,

Who is surrounded by Dragon brood

Your essence is titan and beyond resistance, for you rise as a lion

Shameless in cruelty, hail thou primal father Typhon!

I invoke thee Typhon the hundred headed

I summon thee O coiling drakon of misrule and rebellion!

I invoke thee, Typhon

Whose body is winged to ascend as the Archon-Angel of the Abyss

Whose hands of serpents shall devour those who oppose!

Echidna-Python with Apollo

FROM THE PITS OF TARTARUS

UTTERED BY TYPHON

I called Typhon of old ascend forth from my place of
rest

For here shall I utter the words of power and creation

Zeus and I are one,

As the Mask of the Adversary is of many a visage

With my warcry comes the cries of all wild beasts
together

The serpents which grew from me waved over the
leopard's heads

From the grim lions' manes, coiled as serpents about
the bulls' horns

Let loose the shooting poison mingle with the foam-
spittle of boars

My bright radiance reveals my horror-inspired might
statue!

I am the primal force which shakes the foundations of
the world!

With all my manifold shapes shall I howl forth my
sorceries

Of shadow-tongue vibrated forth in the howling of
wolves

The roaring of cruel lions, the guttural voice of boars

The hissing of serpents, the growling of leopards

The jaws of rearing bears, I am the FURY of the Gods!

I am the terrible and lawless one

Who has joined in union with Ekhidna, the maid with glancing eyes

I have brought forth Orthos the hound of Geryones

Kerberos who eats raw flesh, the brazen-voiced beast of Hades

I have brought forth Khimaira who breathes raging fires

Swift footed and strong, who bears the head of a grim-eyed lion,

A dragon and a goat

I am the master of flesh and the immortal spirit!

The Sphinx who is powerful in the Glory of Egypt!

My bride the worm, she who is of the Serpent

Has brought forth the Kholkian Drakon

The Deathless and unsleeping beast

Hail Gorgon, Daughters of Blackened Fire!

My child the Hydra, who devours and breeds chaos!

Let my wisdom be heard, in any form I take

I shall be as God Eternal!

So it has begun, so it will be done!

EKHIDNA / ECHIDNA

Ekhidna (Echidna) the □rakaina of Delphoi is One Aspect of the Adversary connected with her husband, Typhon. She has the head and breast of a woman yet is a coiling serpent from the waist down. Echidna is the Goddess of the Corruptions of the Earth, the shadow-side or natural course of decay. Echidna is represented as being the presiding power over slime, rot, fetid waters and disease.

It is Hesiod who makes Echidna the daughter of the monstrous sea-gods of primal origin, her powers being of the rotting marshes and places of predatory beasts and reptiles. She is the Queen of Chaos and Darkness, initiatory power and the Bride of the Daimon-Storm God Typhon.

Echidna has immortal power, for Echidna, like Typhon is a Hidden Goddess. In Left hand path mythology and magick lore, Echidna is the as Lilith or Az-Jeh of the Luciferian Path just as Typhon-Set is to Samael and Ahriman.

Echidna is equated in Greek mythology as Python who is the rotting one, a dragon which emerged from the fetid slime after the great Deluge, thus she who arises in power. She sleeps in the dark pit of Tartaros yet ascends still to earth. Enchidna as viewed as half serpent, with speckled skin, eats raw flesh beneath the secret parts of the earth, or Hell (from Helan the secret place or underworld).

Echidna is Python, which Apollo mastered to become a divination God, yet she still dwells in the pits to arise when she wishes. Echidna is also the POENA, a female dragon who was summoned by Apollo to punish Argives. Enchidna, who like Typhon, is immortal. It is written in Hesiod "Theogony" that *"grim Enchidna, a nymph who dies not nor grows old in all her days"*.

Offerings to Echidna should be done in accordance with respect, initiatory workings involving Typhon and the assumption of the left hand path symbolism and magickal ascension. To understand Athena, Demeter or any other beautiful goddess one must fully identify the secret-self with Echidna, as she is equally powerful to understand the self and the possibilities of power.

Typhon

INVOCATION OF ECHIDNA

I call to thee Drakaina of Tartarus

I invoke thee Goddess of the rotting and fetid slime

I exalt thee Echidna who is half-maiden and half-serpent

Whose eyes are black as the pits of Tartarus

Whose eyes flash with the crimson fire of bloodthirsty desire

Mother of Chimaera

Poena, Drakaina of primal hunger

Whose bloodthirsty desire seeks the children in cradles

To drink deep of new life

I summon thee, Goddess of the Serpent-Crown

Whose hands are black and green with decay and death

Whose breasts are spider-veined with rot and corruption

Whose breath is that of fetid swamps

Whose forked tongue instructs the path of power

Who is the mother of Orthus

Whose power is blinding and devouring

Whose dwelled with Typhon in the Caves of Arimi

Who is the Primal Goddess of the land of Scythia

Echidna, Rise up through me and inspire my predatory spirit!

Praise to she whose ghastly hue is reflected from her blackened eyes

Whose breasts are clotted with foul corruption, wherein she devours

Young lives in the web of nightmare!

Whose sharp talons mangle the limbs of the dead

Whose jagged grinding teeth tear forth in nocturnal clamour

Let the howling wolves serve her, who rises up in power!

Echidna, whose strength of Magick is great

Who mouth drips venom, mix the rot with fresh blood

Cast it forth in thy gloomy honor, hail thou Goddess Echidna!

MUS-SAG-IMIN

Mus-sag-imin, the Akkadian seven-headed dragon who battled Ninurta, the God of War, is shown here in battle. This powerful and primal deity was a form of chaos embodied, an early source for Leviathan, Lotan and the Dragon rising from the sea in the book of Revelation. The primal manifestation of the Dragon is a great symbol of chaos, darkness and indeed strength. The primal powers are embodied in serpentine forms, often ravenous and violent in nature. As the gods subdue them, they essential become a higher aspect of their former role. Ninurta, a God who killed the Dragon, becomes a violent a bloodthirsty war-god worshipped by the conquering Assyrian Kings.

MOT

Mot is the God of Death, a son of 'El and who lives in a city called "hmry". His throne is found in a Pit and filth is the land of his heritage. Ba'al warns others that one may not come near to divine death, lest he make you a lamb in his mouth and to be carried away.

Mot himself says his appetite is that of the Lions in the Wilderness and he even has threatened to devour Ba'al himself. Mot had battled ANAT, who splits him in half and burns him, thus she symbolically masters death and is in many considerations "immortal" along with Ba'al.

Luciferians may recognize elements of Mot in the Yatukih-Persian Spirits "Astwihad" and others, for they manifest the transformative elements of death and spiritual continuation.

THE UNDERWORLD AND ABODE

TARTARUS

The primal god of the dark, chaos-pit which lay beneath the foundations of the earth and beneath even the realm of Hades. Tartarus is the pit of darkness, holding no human or anthropomorphic form. Tartarus held the ancient Titans, Gods of Primal Chaos and Abyssic darkness, sealed on all sides with walls of bronze. One may seek to enter into deep trance to communicate the some shades and daimons of Tartarus, however the most productive method if by dream (or nightmare). Light a single black candle before sleep, along with a symbol of Typhon and recite with an offering to the Oneiri. You may hit the ground additionally when calling forth Typhon, when reciting *"Zazas.."* in a frantic, low rhythm.

Tartarus is a place of darkness, or repose and understanding.

Hades enthroned with Cerberus.

AN INVOCATION TO TARTARUS

I seek the wisdom of Typhon

I seek the darkened pit of Tartarus

Open forth God of Primal Darkness

Let my dreaming spirit enter you abode

To gather the knowledge of the forgotten

To rise up again empowered

In darkness and shadows blest

Wide Mouth Chaos OPEN!!!!

I call you by the hidden, forgotten words

ZAZAS, ZAZAS, NASATANADA ZAZAS!!

You may pour a libation into a dark place outside your home, then extinguish candle and retire to bed, with Typhon-Talisman under your pillow.

THE UNDERWORLD OF TYRANNUS IMUS

The Abode of the Dead is a place of gloom and chill-inspired darkness and mist. It is the place of hidden knowledge, for the very word of "Hell" is "Hele" or "to conceal". The practitioners of Luciferian Witchcraft or Sorcery know this place well, as it is their spiritual home for at least part of their initiation.

Past the groves of Persephone lie the Gates of Orcus, or the Mouth of Hades wherein Pluto reigns as king. Those who seek to be brought over the dark waters are led by Kharon or Charon, the primal boat keeper and who was a Daimon of Death in Etruscan mythology.

Poplars and willows grow along with Asphodel in the land of the dead, near the Gates of Hades. The shades of the dead go forth in various manifestations. The spirits of the dead sought to drink the blood of the dead, for it nourished them.

Kerberos rests at the portal to hell, for he is gigantic and covered with the mane of serpents. The dense mists of Tartarus enshrouds all in Hades, there is no end to the darkness and tunnels there, for Tartarus is the abode of abyssic darkness, the most terrible predatory daimons rest there, waiting to hear the call of blood and life, to rise up again to manifest in the world of the living.

Akheron or Acheron is the God of the Underworld river of darkness in which Charon or Kharon guides souls across, for it too runs past the site of the ancient

Necromanteion, the place where one conducts rites of communication with the shades of the dead. The wife of the river-god Acheron was Orphne and Gorgyra, who was a nymph who manifests throughout the underworld.

Another underworld river of tears and wailing is called Kokytos or Cocytus. This river is considered a "god" as well. Styx is the Underworld River of Hate and Vengence, whose streams encircle the realm of the dead. Gods often swore solemn oaths by the pitch-black waters of the abyss.

Luciferian practitioners may seek these waters to gain inner knowledge, allow their own shades to drink of these waters. The one river which should be avoided is LETHE, who manifests as the Goddess of the River of Oblivion. Only the Shades of the dead who wish to forget their former lives should drink from it, for no doubt they are soon consumed by vampiric shades. The Infernal River of Fire is Pyriphlegethon and will inspire the Shades with Immortal Consciousness (the Black Fire of Azazel) or consume shades entirely in its destroying fires.

The Throne of Hades is a haunting place. The court surrounding Hades is made of three judges of the dead, Erinyes, Keres, Moirai and Black Mors called Thanatos, Stygian Juno or Persephone. The Judges seek to know if you have lived consistently with your values, done well by others and not proven a coward. This is the judgment of the Shade itself, for you know within your own heart your value.

V.   MOON PHASES AND WITCHCRAFT

The Cycle of the Moon and Workings

Some may view Luciferian Paganism as being connected with instinct, balancing it with nature. Others utilize Magick and connect with the current via ritual practice. Others use both in a balanced way to strength and increase awareness in life.

I invoke thee Ba'al Berit who
brings power to the strong
and wise
By the powers of the Sea,
Hail thou God of the Depths
Whose cult was revered ages ago
Highest of the Gods,
Lord of the Sea
Ba'al Berit of the Golden Trident

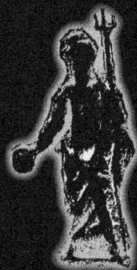

Helios, crown of the Sun
Who shines upon humanity
and the Immortal Gods
Whose piercing gaze
sends light with his eyes
Gazing triumphantly with
his Golden Helmet

MOON WORKINGS AND EXAMPLES

Those interested in the system of Luciferian Witchcraft may observe and celebrate the Goddess and Gods from the following instances.

FULL MOON

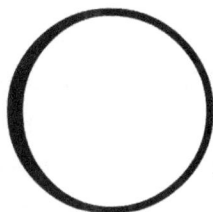

The energy associated with the Full Moon is the power and clarity of the self made aware through your own initiatory experience. The Full Moon is a time of honoring the Goddess and God as a divinatory working of knowing yourself, increasing psychic energy and building the spiritual energy associated. You may begin Hecate workings of honoring the Goddess three days prior, the third ending on the Full Moon night.

The Luciferian Witchcraft associated with Hecate is the Goddess in her most beautiful aspect, she is the striking huntress, the pale and dark goddess who with a smile brings you close and if you're afraid of your instincts or unsure of yourself – become impaled on the horns of her Therionick (or beast like) nature.

You may visualize Hecate in her traditional form and draw the energy into yourself. Traditional witches call this "Drawing down the Moon" however the Luciferian tradition offers numerous avenues of exploring the nature of the Goddess and even God from a full moon perspective.

GODDESSES, GODS ASSOCIATED WITH FULL MOON:

Hecate – Crimson is her color as the Mother phase, she is the summer beauty of full womanhood or the nurturing Dark Goddess who awakens instinct and predatory nature.

Diana, Pan, Dionysos are examples of energies which may be evoked via the Full Moon. Zeus as the Wolf God, Apollo as the Destroying Wolf as well is meaningful in dream magick and associative sorceries. Offering to Ares/Mars would also be instructive in undertaking a choice battle or conflict to achieve resolution.

NEW (Dark) MOON

The new moon is generally utilized for growth and self-determined direction. The crone or hag is renewed with youth and vigor, she is the Maiden awakened. This is the spring, the time of dawn and youth.

Invoking or Offering to start a new focus or process is best used with a new moon. White is the color associated with the new moon.

Gods and Goddess associated with the New Moon are Hecate as Maiden, Tyche, Apollo, Zeus the Lightning God, Bendis are suitable examples.

If working with dark currents, you may use the Dark Moon to evoke energies of Typhon, Hecate, Apollyon the Destroyer, Dionysos the Madness Bringer for insight and individual strengthening of the senses.

WAXING MOON

Attraction and sexual magick is the best period for working in this phase, between the Dark and Full Moon.

Invoke the Goddess as Maiden yet also God forms such as Apollo the Music-God, Dionysos, Pan and other seductive youthful Gods and Goddesses.

WANING MOON

Called sometimes the Waning Moon, this is the time of darkness and chthonic sorceries dedicated to the shadow. Not to be confused with a negative, the phase of the Mother transformed into Hag and the death-daimons which instruct us on dreams and nightmares. We may focus on what we wish to grow from and understand that darkness is a beautiful aspect within each of us.

Invoking Typhon and Echidna for getting in touch with your beast-like aspect, working with Hades to understand your deep desires, communication with the shades of the dead and exploring the vampyric aspects of the astral plane. Poseidon may be offered to in understanding dreams and evoking the primal.

Apollyon the King of the Bottomless Pit, Far-Striker, Zeus as the Serpent, Typhon, Echidna, Hecate as Crone, Hades and Persephone, Dionysos the God of Dark Sexuality, Poseidon and others may be offered to accordingly.

THEURGY AND TRANSFORMATION

The Great Work of Theurgy is the "divine working" which is from a left hand path or Luciferian perspective, is similar to the process known as "Azal'ucel" or the Divine Higher aspects of self.

This process alone does not necessarily represent any exterior force or supplication rather recognizing this spiritual communion within the self or embodied soul of the Magickian or Luciferian.

GOETIA

Basic later "Sorcery", the process of encircling or channeling spirits or daimonic energy into a specific area for a purpose, to gain wisdom, love, revenge, protection, wealth or otherwise earthly gains. Yatukih Sorcery and Therionick Sorcery in Luciferianism fit partially into this category.

THEURGY

Adapted from Lamblichus and other forms of Neoplatonism, Theurgy from a Luciferian perspective aims at communion with the Adversarial Spirit – called Archon or the unity of Samael – Lilith to beget the higher force, or Angel in man and woman. Within the context of Luciferian Paganism presented in this book, it may either be Zeus and Hera, the Conquering force which relates also to Hecate, Apollo, Dionysos, Cybele, etc as well as Typhon and Echidna, the shadow aspect. Neither one is considered Good or Evil. Darkness and Chaos is a creative force as well as destructive.

Consider the actions of the Gods, have they not dealt well in the works of Chaos and Darkness as much as of Order and Light? Without one, the other may not fall into place.

Theurgy is the work of gaining communion with your instinctual self – the shadow, or hungering "body" aspect as well as the angelic or "higher" aspect of the "mind" and "spirit".

The work presented here within the chapters "Theos Epiphanes" and "Theoi Khthonioi" are exact grimoires of Theurgy and attaining higher ascension of self. Within those works, the "Goetic" or "Sorcerous" works of the body and fleshly life are plainly demonstrated with the basic attributes of the Gods.

A NOTE ON MAGICK AND PRACTICE

Understanding nature and the role of Magick is essential for any practitioner who is aware of their own life. Nature holds a key to our understanding of the forces within us. We live in the world touched and shaped by experiences, think of how you alone have been affected by your experiences from a child onward. We must be completely aware that we must look to each experience as something which can strengthen us, offer perspective or *potentially weaken us* if we let it.

Magick is about ascension, becoming someone strong, wise and powerful. Darkness and light are balanced and equally enlightening. Often, it takes a journey into darkness to come forth bearing light.

THE PROCESS OF THEURGIC RITUALS

You should initially gain your experience with basic offerings to the Gods and find which ones resonate with you the most. Once done and when you are comfortable, you should seek to begin rituals and prayers to gain communion and then self-transformation.

Don't overcomplicate the initial process, as a Luciferian you may seek to commune with the Gods in terms of offerings to achieve insight. Over time you may find yourself seeking more – a union of the Olympian or Chthonic, where if so you should seek the next step which is the process of continual self-transformation.

There are numerous ways and methods to achieve the Theurgic Communion, in Luciferian Witchcraft and Adversarial Magick traditions there is *"The Ritual of Azal'ucel[1]"* and *"Daemonum Magna Mater"[2]*, to achieve communion with the Daemonic Angelic Force, or higher instinct of self.

You may wish to use the Invocations within this grimoire to that end as well, don't be afraid to be creative and utilize your imagination. Listening to INSTINCTS is always the right step – this is how one gains communion with the Higher Self.

Once you conduct the workings and achieve this communion, it is not over. Initiation is a life-long

---

[1] THE BIBLE OF THE ADVERSARY – 2007 Succubus Productions.

[2] AKHKHARU – Vampyre Magick 2008 Succubus Productions.

journey and a continual Adversarial process of self-transformation.

At the end of life the process of shedding the body, ascending as a Luciferian or Ahrimanic Spirit, is a process of self-deification and becoming divine. The normal consciousness is tended to be shed and a new aspect of being arises. This is a part of the great mystery and should be a side-line focus compared to your life here and now. After all, it is what we do with our life, experience and knowledge which transforms us as who we are and the potential therein.

The significance of Paganism from a Luciferian perspective is found in the difference of perception from not only traditional occult elements – yet also traditional "Satanic" ones as well. You are challenged to interpret it differently and based on your own individuality. Obviously, how you apply this system or manifest the Gods in your life will dictate your results in the end.

DREAM RISING

A Deific Mask within the Luciferian tradition is a energy or God form "masked" in an anthropomorphic form, given a visage in which you can relate to. Some Pagans will seek to work with specific Gods or Goddesses to better understand and utilize their power in their own life. There are some simple techniques in which to do this.

Planning to adopt a God Form or Deific Mask in the dream plane may be a suitable way to start understanding this power and how it manifests in your life. With knowledge and experience comes wisdom, the very Eucharist of Luciferianism – the power to shape your life!

Visualize an image of the God, what you wish to gain knowledge of during the day before night comes. Once you have done this, offer some incense at the altar of this God or Goddess during the day.

Complicated Gods or Goddesses with many epithets should be worked with simplistically, for instance with Zeus one may utilize the Deific Mask of Zeus Nikephorus as being the God of your personal victory of a situation. This could be a job promotion, overcoming a particular challenge or such. Seek the imagery of this Deific Mask in the form associated with Zeus Nikephorus.

If the God is Typhon or Hecate, your power and knowledge sought will be more hidden, or subtle in relation to primal desire. Visualize this power representing a hunger for mastering your problems and using those more subtle, dark or "predatory" instincts to achieve success.

Here are some steps to enter the dreaming plane.

1. Visualizing the Deific Mask in an anthropomorphic form before sleep, offering again incense at the altar with a simple mantra:

   I seek the God/dess ...name... to enter me, cloak me in the form of my desire and I shall go forth and gain knowledge of your divinity.

2. Close your eyes and visualize your spirit taking the form of this God/dess or deific mask – see your self standing outside your body.

3. Go forth towards your goal and allow yourself to fall asleep.

4. Upon waking, write down your observations and recollection before you forget. If little is remembered don't worry – often knowledge will manifest from the subconscious later on with visions, further dreams, impulses or in art, writing or some form of expression. Listen to your instinct and you will be surprised what you can achieve.

THE RITE OF OPENING

A basic opening invocation to clear the mind and focus on the rite itself. Ritual workings are times of drawing as one with the Deific Mask you seek, it is not just a supplication towards a higher power. In every work, you are transforming yourself into that higher power, the only God or Goddess that is. This is by the point that all deific powers, angels, demons or abyssic phantasms will communicate through you, your sense will perceive them and offering a mask for their manifestation. Learn much and gain power from each working.

I light this candle

In the willed assumption of self-deification

I light this candle

In the name of the ancient powers

Be it male, female, all knowing and illuminated

Be present unto and through me

For I am the only God or Goddess that is

You are most alive in me as in nature

I light this candle in honor of the Blackened Flame

That which brought the wisdom of Dionysos, the serpents of self-knowing

Gather here and without guilt I take

The Love and power in which we celebrate!

Sphinx, the offspring of Typhon and Echidna.

ILLUMINATING THE WATER

Take Athame and plunge the tip into the cup:

I illuminate the as the fulguris lightening flash

O Ancient Gods and Goddesses of Water

O Daimon of Water, Poseidon

Lend me the power of the Trident!

O Ba'al Berit God of Wealth and Power

I conjure thee to unite the Above and Sacred

Depths of Darkness and Light

Of the world of phantasm and strengthening light

CASTING THE CIRCLE

The circle as mentioned here may be as simple or as elaborate as you wish. In traditional Luciferian Witchcraft rites, the circle represents the self, the very daemonic forces being leant from the depths of the subconscious and nature itself. You may wish to correspond such within the Olympian and Chthonic gods here as well.

Using flour is a useful ingredient in circle casting outdoors, simply start in the north and move widdershins or anti-clockwise to complete the circle. You may visualize the circle as well or utilize a premade cloth or boundary stones placed at the respective directions.

I ensorcel thee, O circle of power and primordial shadow

Thou is the boundary of self, of possibility and wisdom!

Thou is a meeting place of the crossroads

Sacred unto Hekate and her power of darkness

And phantasmic shades

This circle is my place of sanctuary and where my Will is made flesh

Never shall I cower within it or use it to shield that which I call forth!

Never shall I hold the powers within or outside at bay!

For I am of the serpent path, against those servants of sheep and weakened gods

For I am in flesh God Manifest!

I raise the power as the spiral force of chaos made order

Shadow intertwined with Light and all masks of my making!

I consecrate thee!

BIBLIOGRAPHY

Prolegomena to the study of Greek Religion by Jane Ellen Harrison

The Gods of Greece and Rome by Talfourd Ely

Homer, The Iliad - Greek Epic C9th-8th BC

Hesiod, Shield of Heracles - Greek Epic C8th-7th BC

Hesiod, THEOGONY translated by H.G. Eveyln-White

The Homeric Hymns - Greek Epic C8th-4th BC

Ovid, Metamorphoses - Latin Epic C1st BC - C1st AD

A History of Secret Societies Akron Daraul

LAROUSSE "WORLD MYTHOLOGY" 1965

THEOI . COM – an exceptional source of mythological material

GLOSSARY

ASANA – Posture relating to the practice of Yoga. In reference to the Luciferian Path, posture is anything which is steady or consistent. There is no defined posture in Ahrimanic Yoga, although there are suggestions.

ATAVISM – A beast-like subconscious memory of knowledge, a pre-human aspect of the subconscious –the serpent, crocodile or other reptilian form. Atavisms are often latent power points in the mind.

AZOTHOZ – A sigillic word formula which represent the Golden Dawn definition of the Beginning and End, Alpha and Omega. Azothoz is a reversed form which is a symbol and glyph of the Adversary, Shaitan/Set and Lilith. This is a word which signifies self-initiation and the power which is illuminated by the Black Flame within.

Black Flame – The Gift of Shaitan/Set, being individual perception and deific consciousness. The Black Flame or Black Light of Iblis is the gift of individual awakening which separates the magician from the natural universe, being an Antinomian gift of Luciferian perception. The Black Flame is strengthened by the initiation of the Black Adept, who is able to balance a spiritual path with the physical world.

Black Magick – The practice of Antinomian and self-focused transformation, self-deification and the obtainment of knowledge and wisdom. Black Magick in itself does not denote harm or wrongdoing to others, rather describes "black" as considered to the Arabic root word FHM, charcoal, black and wisdom. Black is thus the color of hidden knowledge. Magick is to ascend and become, by Willed focus and direction.

Daeva [Avestan/Pahlavi] – demons, those who are children of Ahriman and Az. Daeva also makes reference to "Spirit" of Ahriman, those who have walked the path of the serpent, i.e. antinomianism or the left hand path.

Daimon [Greek] – Denotes Spirit, a spiritual being which exists with isolate intelligence. Each man or woman in Luciferianism has a Daimon and is not related or separated from a Kako-Daimon, evil spirit or Agathos-Daimon, or Good Spirit. Luciferian recognize balance.

DEIFIC MASK – A symbol of anthropomorphic assumption of a God as a figure, the manifestation of a specific deity or power.

Evil Eye – In the old Gathic writings, the Evil Eye is considered a power of the Daeva and Druj, meaning the power to cause death, oppression and sickness. In a modern sense, the Evil Eye represents the window to the Soul or Spirit itself, not merely as a negative but equally so a positive. The Eye of the Yatu is the commanding presence which is a form of spell casting, to focus the Will itself on the desired goal, to achieve a result. Many Daevas are directly related to the Evil Eye, thus is as well a symbol of Ahriman.

Left Hand Path – The Antinomian (*against the current, natural order*) path which leads through self-deification (godhood). LHP signifies that humanity has an intellect which is separate from the natural order, thus in theory and practice may move forward with seeking the mastery of the spirits (referring to the elements of the self) and controlled direction in a positive area of ones own life – the difference between RHP is they seek union with the universe, nirvana and bliss. The LHP seeks disunion to grow in perception and being, strength and the power of an awakened mind. The Left Hand Path from the Sanskrit Vama Marga, meaning 'Left Way', symbolizes a path astray all others, subjective only to itself. To truly walk upon the Left Hand Path, one must strive to break all personal taboos and gain knowledge and power from this averse way, thus expand power accordingly.

Lilith [Hebrew]– The Goddess of Witchcraft, Magick and Sorcery. Lilith was the first wife of Adam who refused to be submission and joined with the shadows and demonic spirits in the deserts. Lilith was also said to be the spiritual mother of Cain by her mate, Samael (Shaitan) the Dragon. Lilith appeared in Sumerian times as a Goddess of the Beasts of the Wild, as well as Sorcery and Night-fornication. Lilith was said to have many forms, from beautiful women to half human and the bottom half animal, to half woman and half flame. Lilith is also the mother of demons and a Vampyric spirit which is a primal manifestation of the Zoroastrian and Manichaean AZ and Jeh. Lilith may also be related to the Indian KALI, whose name is one of Her 17 names.

Luciferian – A Luciferian is an individual who recognizes the associative spiritual traits of the God/ess within. Luciferians do not worship Satan but recognize there must be balance between the material and spiritual, the darkness and light. Luciferians view their own being as holding the Black Flame of Lucifer – Samael and Lilith within, this is intellect and wisdom. This is beyond good and evil, the spirit has two aspects – the demonic (instinct, desire) and angelic (intelligence, consciousness).

Luciferian Magick – Essentially close to the term, Black Magick but specifically focuses on ascending in a self-deified and isolated way in reference to Lucifer, the bringer of Light. Luciferian Magick may in this term make reference to seeking Light and darkness through magickal development, not an abstract concept, but to manifest the Will in both the spiritual and physical world.

Magick - To Ascend and Become. In a Luciferian sense, Magick is to strengthen, develop and initiate the self through balanced forms of Willed Change.

Predatory Spiritualism – The act of devouring spiritual energy and making the Adept stronger from ritual practice, the act of encircling spiritual energy either symbolically or literally based on theistic or non-theistic belief, once encircling the spirit or deific mask, symbolically devouring and consuming the association of the spirit into the self. May be attributed to the inner practices of the Black Order of the Dragon. A ritual published in Luciferian Witchcraft, The Ritual of Druj Nasu is a vampiric or predatory rite utilizing ancient Persian sorcery inversions and techniques of sorcery for strengthening consciousness.

Sabbat – The gathering and conclave of sorcerers. There are in a conceptual sense, two types of Sabbats – the Luciferian and the Infernal. The Infernal is a bestial and earth-bound journey, similar to those shown in woodcuts and gathering points. The Infernal Sabbat is sometimes sexual, where the sorcerer may shape shift and communicate with their familiars and spirits. The Luciferian Sabbat is a solar and air phenomena based in dreaming, floating in air and having sensations of a warm heat similar to sitting out in the sun. The Luciferian Sabbat is a strengthening and development of the Body of Light, the astral double of the Adept.

Sabbatic – A term which is related as the knowledge of the secret gathering, the Sabbat. This is a focus of inspired teaching based on magickal development via dreaming and astral projection. The Sabbat is the gathering of sorcerers in dreaming flesh, when the body is shed for the psyche which is able to go forth in whatever form it desires. The witch or sorcerer who is able to attend the Sabbat has already freed the mind through a process of Antinomian magical practice, thus enforcing and strengthening the imagination as a visualization tool, similar to divination and 'sight' with spirits.

Shades – Spirits of the Dead, ghosts and phantoms which walks in the astral plane. These spirits may represent in some cases the body of the sorcerer in the plane of the dead, a world separate in some areas from our own living perception. In evocation and necromantical practice, the shades are brought around and closer to the world of the living.

Sorcery – The art of encircling energy and power of self, by means of self -fascination (inspiration through the imagination). Sorcery is a willed controlling of energies of a magical current, which is responsive through the Will and Belief of the sorcerer. While sorcery is the encircling or ensorcerling of power around the self, Magick is the Willed change of ones objective universe.

Staota [Avestan/Pahlavi] – A Vibration which could cause death or some change, that which would encircle the one sounding the Staota in self-focused energy. A Staota is used historically in the mythological tale, The Matigan-I Yosht-I Fryan. A Sorcerous technique presented in the Second Edition of YATUK DINOIH.

Therion [Greek] – The Beast Refers to the hidden aspects of the mind. Inner desires and the subconscious force which manifests in often animalistic or bestial forms (i.e. demons).

Vampirism/Vampyrism – The act of consuming Chi or Anghuya in a ritualized setting. Life or energy force is found in all things; the sorcerer practicing vampirism would encircle and consume to grow stronger with this energy. Practitioners of Vampirism DO create their own Chi but also use Chi absorbed or drained from other sources to manipulate the shadow by dream and ritual, growing stronger. The Eye is both a symbol of vampirism and Luciferian practice, predatory spirituality. Vampirism is based in the foundations of early Egyptian texts and Charles Darwin theories of natural selection. Not referring to the Religion of Vampirism. See PREDATORY SPIRITUALISM.

DEDICATION

I would like to dedicate the book to Douglas Grant of Dagon Productions, who supported and sold my work in the early days as well as Nathaniel Harris. In addition, a special thank you to the initiates of The Order of Phosphorus and Black Order of the Dragon. To Antiochus IV Epiphanes, Emperor Nero, Emperor Domitian and Julius Flavius who fought the restrictions of ignorance, Judeo-Christian intolerance and to keep the beauty and strength of the Gods alive in humanity. I want to thank Hope Marie for her dedication and support. In addition, Nathaniel Harris, initiates of The Order of Phosphorus and all of those who have supported this work. Thank you to Kindra Ravenmoon and Draconis as well.

MICHAEL W. FORD has been a practicing Luciferian and Satanist for over 16 years. A Luciferian, Yatukih magickian, Michael has work in the areas of Luciferian Witchcraft, Left Hand Path magick, Yatuk-Dinoih or ancient Persian sorcery, Typhonian Magick, Chaos Sorcery, Nocturnal Spiritual Vampyrism and more. Ford has also founded the Black Order of the Dragon and The Order of Phosphorus, currently presiding as Magus over both orders. Mr. Ford lives currently in Texas and is co-owner of the Luciferian Apotheca, a popular left hand path magickal shop found at www.luciferianwitchcraft.com

www.ingramcontent.com/pod-product-compliance
Lightning Source LLC
Chambersburg PA
CBHW020607270326
41927CB00005B/221